Carry the Cross with Padre Pio

"Prepare yourself to embark on a spiritually transformative Lenten journey with St. Padre Pio, one of the most beloved saints of our time. *Carry the Cross with Padre Pio: Daily Devotions for Lent* is a true Lenten treasure you will want to pick up year after year. This fantastic book offers readers a daily opportunity to unlock spiritual insights and teachings from Padre Pio, read insightful reflections by Susan De Bartoli, and meditate on prayers that will help you grow in your faith. Read this book for a life-impacting Lent."

Emily Jaminet
Author of *Secrets of the Sacred Heart*

"Every year, as Lent approaches, my heart wavers between dread and excitement. Is this another Lent where I will make a million promises and see none through? This year, however, I have Susan De Bartoli's simple, in-depth, and truly inspirational devotional, guided by one of our modern spiritual giants—Padre Pio. With short reflections and rich content, De Bartoli's devotional gives me hope for experiencing a Lent well lived."

Allison Gingras
Author of *Encountering Signs of Faith*

"Susan De Bartoli takes us through another season of the liturgical calendar through the lens of Padre Pio, for whom almost every day was Lent. As with *Welcoming the Christ Child with Padre Pio: Daily Reflections for*

Advent, Carry the Cross with Padre Pio is a wonderful way to reflect on the meaning of our Lord's sacrifice."

Corrie Campbell
Chief Development Officer
National Centre for Padre Pio

"Susan De Bartoli takes us on a unique, day-by-day journey through Lent using her comprehensive knowledge of Padre Pio's life and in-depth understanding of his spirituality. Each page of this book gives us a new spiritual insight from Padre Pio that will deepen your faith."

Julie Fitts Ritter
Executive Director
Padre Pio Foundation of America

Carry the Cross with Padre Pio

Daily Reflections for Lent

Susan De Bartoli

AVE MARIA PRESS AVE Notre Dame, Indiana

© 2025 by Susan De Bartoli

All rights reserved. No part of this book may be used or reproduced in any manner whatsoever, except in the case of reprints in the context of reviews, without written permission from Ave Maria Press®, Inc., P.O. Box 428, Notre Dame, IN 46556, 1-800-282-1865.

Founded in 1865, Ave Maria Press is a ministry of the United States Province of Holy Cross.

www.avemariapress.com

Paperback: ISBN-13 978-1-64680-383-5

E-book: ISBN-13 978-1-64680-384-2

Cover image © Tom Crehan, Darling Beads of May.

Cover and text design by Christopher D. Tobin.

Printed and bound in the United States of America.

Library of Congress Cataloging-in-Publication Data is available.

Contents

Foreword

Francesco Forgione (1887–1968), better known as Padre Pio, was a Capuchin monk and mystic who waged a life-long battle for the souls of his spiritual children and whose extraordinary spiritual gifts made demons tremble. To this day, Padre Pio ranks high in the echelon of saints known all over the world, alongside St. Francis of Assisi and St. Thérèse of Lisieux, as an intercessor who always answers the phone.

When I was the rector of the Pontifical North American College in Rome, I discovered just how popular Padre Pio is as an intercessory when my niece, Shannon, was diagnosed with cancer. One of the Italian workers would frequently ask me how she was doing, and I asked him to pray to Jesus for her. "Oh, I don't pray to Jesus," he said. "I always go right to Padre Pio!" While one might argue with his Christology, I was deeply touched by his confidence in the wonder-working saint.

Perhaps the most impressive miracle Jesus worked through Padre Pio was his ability to read the human heart. At the height of his ministry, he sat in the confessional twelve to fifteen hours a day, hearing over forty thousand confessions each year. His irascible manner did not endear him to everyone and, like a veteran surgeon wielding a scalpel, his no-nonsense approach quickly cut to the heart of every matter.

At Padre Pio's beatification, I met an Italian-American veteran who had gone to see Padre Pio after World War II, determined to see the Stigmata on Pio's hands. After Mass, as Padre Pio came to greet him, the soldier demanded, "Show me your wounds." Calmly, the old priest turned the greeting back on him. "Show me *yours*." Baffled, the soldier wondered what he was talking about. "We all have wounds," the Capuchin explained. "We all have the wounds of the Cross—mine just happen to be visible. But you are carrying some too. I can see them. Come with me." Leading the weeping soldier into the confessional, Padre Pio learned that he had left two wounded buddies in a foxhole in order to save himself. The weight of his guilt was unbearable—until at last Padre Pio showed him how to lay it down.

As the author of the bestseller *Welcoming the Christ Child with Padre Pio* and secretary of the Board of Directors for the Padre Pio Foundation of America, Susan De Bartoli has a gift for communicating the charisms and gifts of her favorite saint with simplicity and profound faith. In *Welcoming the Christ Child with Padre Pio*, she captures the intimate friendship Padre Pio experienced with the Blessed Mother and the Christ Child. In *Welcoming the Holy Spirit with Padre Pio*, Susan introduces his mystical and supernatural gifts in order to show how we, too, can serve the Lord with all our hearts, as Padre Pio did.

In this, her third book about Padre Pio, she dives deep into the heart of his letters to show both his humanity and fidelity. She gives us a glimpse into the life of someone who understood what it means to carry the Cross with Jesus. That cross took many forms over the course of his lifetime—physical and mental sufferings, isolations, rejections, and frightening visions. His letters to his spiritual directors reveal how he was able to endure it all, consoled and strengthened by the invisible hands of his Guardian Angel and the Blessed Mother. Whether you read this book during Lent or simply during times of personal struggle, you will get to know through this great saint both the consolations and desolations of following Jesus along the via dolorosa . . . all the way to Easter joy.

+ Cardinal Timothy M. Dolan
Archbishop of New York

Introduction

St. Pio of Pietrelcina (Padre Pio, 1887–1968) is one of the most beloved and revered of the twenty-first-century saints. Dozens of books have been written about this Capuchin mystic and miracle worker and his extraordinary spiritual gifts.

In this book, we see another side of Padre Pio: spiritual father, warrior, and most of all beloved son of the Heavenly Father. Because of the difficulty of the work God had given him to do, Padre Pio was given special graces, including visits from the angelic hosts as well as the Blessed Mother herself.

On this Lenten journey to Easter, we follow the path that Padre Pio walked, a path that leads to Calvary. We listen to Padre Pio's stories of dark nights and glorious mornings. We witness his Mass through the eyes of those who attended. Each day, we'll read Lenten reflections and discover the wisdom of Padre Pio through his letters to his spiritual directors, enriching our own spiritual journey. Through Padre Pio's suffering, we begin to understand how much Jesus suffered for us. Padre Pio partook of this journey knowing and accepting all that he would suffer for the love of Our Lord, Jesus Christ.

This Lenten devotional offers a unique glimpse into the highs and lows of this great Capuchin's spiritual journey. Each week consists of five reflections on the struggles and sufferings of Padre Pio—a kind of "way of the Cross"—followed by a sixth reflection on the consolations he received, to keep him strong as he journeyed toward Easter. As any good Father, the Lord recognizes our human weaknesses and limits, and within our sufferings he offers moments of hope and respite. For Padre Pio, these moments often took the form of heavenly visitations from Mary and the angels and saints. At times, the Lord himself would come alongside Padre Pio and strengthen him. And in doing so, God reminds each of us that he never leaves us alone in our dark nights, even though (because of our own limitations) we cannot always sense him near.

So, before we begin our journey, following in the footsteps of Padre Pio as he follows Jesus on the path of redemption, let's take a personal inventory and consider what cross the Lord is asking us to carry, for love of him, as we all journey toward Easter. Consider sharing your thoughts with your confessor (as Padre Pio often did) or in a letter to Jesus in your journal. Without suffering, there can be no healing, no redemption. Experiencing Jesus's suffering on this journey to Calvary helps us grasp how we can find healing through our own suffering. Jesus bore our pain and sorrows, walking with them on his path to Calvary. He lifts us up, carrying our crosses alongside us and easing our burdens. Through his suffering, we are healed, and through his Crucifixion and death, we are redeemed.

The road to Calvary is marked by suffering, and as we journey with Padre Pio, we begin to understand how the Lord embraced our pain to bring us healing. Redemption means being healed from sin. Take a moment now to thank the Lord for the journey of love ahead as we walk together toward the glories of Easter.

All for the Love of His Childhood Companion

Week of Ash Wednesday

Pick Up Your Cross

> The life and mission of Padre Pio testify that difficulties and sorrows, if accepted with love, transform themselves into a privileged journey of holiness, which opens the person toward a greater good, known only to the Lord.
>
> —St. John Paul II, homily at the canonization of Padre Pio, 2002

For Catholics, Ash Wednesday is a day on which we recognize our human frailty. The ashes on our foreheads are a visible reminder of our faith. The ashes mark the beginning of forty days when we will contemplate Christ's sacrifice, Death, and Resurrection. This is a joyful journey because it passes through Calvary and leads us into Easter morning!

In the Mass, we celebrate how Christ redeemed us through his Passion and Death. It is a joyful event. Yes, as we pick up our crosses, we know there will be suffering and sorrow, but when we arrive at Easter, we will feel the joy of the redeemed Christ in our hearts.

For Padre Pio—and for all of us—every day is a "little Lent," another step toward holiness as we offer up and unite our sufferings and sacrifices to Christ our Redeemer.

In the following letter dated February 1, 1915, Padre Pio tells his spiritual director, Padre Agostino, that the demons had urged Padre Pio to tear up his confessor's letters without reading them. At first, Padre Pio chose to remain silent, not responding to the temptation. Then the demons flung themselves upon Padre Pio like many hungry tigers. Yet he was not frightened, Padre Pio told his confessor, for by his love Jesus "has followed me everywhere" (*Letters I*, 377). On February 1, 1913, he writes:

> Jesus tells me that in love it is he who delights me, while in suffering, on the other hand, it is I who give him pleasure. Now, to desire good health would mean seeking happiness for myself instead of trying to comfort Jesus. Yes, I love the Cross, the Cross alone; I love it because I always see it on Jesus' shoulders. By this time Jesus is well aware that my entire life, my whole heart, is consecrated to Him and his sufferings. . . .
>
> I realize that I made him suffer exceedingly by my failings, that I made him weep . . . by my ingratitude, that I have offended Him grievously. I want nobody but Jesus, I desire nothing else (which is Jesus' own desire) than his sufferings. Allow me to say it, since no one can hear us, . . . I am ready even to be deprived forever of the tenderness which Jesus lavishes on me, I am prepared to bear His hiding His beautiful eyes from me as long as He does not hide from me His love,

for this would cause me death. But I could not bear to
be deprived of suffering. I lack the strength for this.
(*Letters I*, 376)

Reflect

Jesus wants us to join him on this path to Calvary so that
we can understand how much God loves us! By taking up
our crosses patiently, we have an opportunity to return
a bit of that love to him. Through prayer and fasting, we
can share this journey with Padre Pio along the path that
Jesus took to Calvary.

How can we trust in God's providence to uphold us
not only during Lent but throughout all the difficult times
that follow? Reflect on the following words of Padre Pio:

> Take concern to have your heart be more pleasing to
> our Master day by day. Do things in such a way that the
> current year will be more fruitful in good works than
> the last. The years are passing by, and we are approach-
> ing eternity, so we need to redouble our courage and
> lift our souls up to God, serving him with more dili-
> gence in everything that our Christian vocation or pro-
> fession requires of us. This alone can make us pleasing
> to God. . . . Only this can enable us to arrive at the gate
> of eternal salvation.[1]

Christ, My Redeemer . . .

Through the life of Padre Pio, I see how you comfort
us in affliction, sustain us in danger, and watch over us
with your grace so that we might make our way safely to

heaven. Draw me close to your Divine Heart, that one day I would be worthy of Paradise. Amen.

Conclude your time of reflection and prayer with one Our Father, one Hail Mary, and one Glory Be.

I Am a Mystery to Myself

> There lives here in a cold and small monastery a competitor of St. Francis of Assisi, who is named Padre Pio, and his hands and feet are pierced by the Stigmata. Every morning, he celebrates Mass before sunrise, when the peasants begin to go to work in the fields. All his daily life is an example of humility and dedication to his Lord; he scorns worldly goods and considers supreme only the love [of] Christ.
>
> —Mary Pyle, in a letter to her mother

In order to take this journey, we must first understand something of the man who is leading us. Understanding Padre Pio poses a significant challenge. Padre Pio said, "What can I tell you about me? I am a mystery to myself!"[2] All we know and can explain is that Padre Pio lived like the Crucified Christ and had a profound devotion to both Jesus and Mary.

As a true spiritual teacher, Padre Pio used his incredible gifts to form souls who were in love with God and nourished by the wisdom of the Cross. By his great examples and words, many followed him—including his dear spiritual daughter, American heiress Mary Pyle, who continually opened her home near San Giovanni to those who thronged to receive his counsel and blessing.

Padre Pio recognized his calling as a chosen instrument of God, uniting his entire life to Christ's redemptive mission through love and embracing the Cross. In a June 1913 letter to Padre Benedetto, his spiritual director, Padre Pio shared his desire to follow Jesus even in martyrdom.

> [My] soul goes on fire with the most keen desire to possess Jesus entirely. Then, with an indescribable vividness communicated to my soul by the Lord, I am shown as in a mirror my whole future life as nothing but a martyrdom. Without knowing why, and with unspeakable love, I yearn for death. Despite all my efforts I am driven to ask God with tears in my eyes let me be taken from this exile. I feel inflamed with such a lively and ardent desire to please God, and am gripped by such a fear of falling into any slightest imperfection that I would like to flee from all dealings with creatures. However, another desire rises up like a giant in my heart, the longing to be in the midst of all people to proclaim at the top of my voice who this great God of mercy is. (*Letters I*, 413)

Reflect

The life Padre Pio chose was full of sacrifices, which he saw as acts of love. Padre Pio joyfully embraced all bodily suffering, discerning God's calling within his heart to increase his self-sacrifices for the sake of others.

Padre Pio lived his whole life thinking about the Cross, wanting to make God happy, becoming a better person, and helping others find salvation. He learned everything from Jesus, who always followed what God the Father wanted with love and without hesitation. He saw the value in earthly sufferings, which he believed lead us to an everlasting eternity with the Lord.

We all have crosses in life. Padre Pio teaches us how to bear our crosses well and offer all that we suffer through them for our salvation. Reflect on these words of Padre Pio:

> One day, when we are granted to see the full noon-day light, we will recognize and value, how great is the treasure that we earned from our earthly sufferings for the homeland that will have no end. From generous souls and from those in love, God expects acts of heroism and fidelity so that, after the ascent of Calvary, they may reach Mount Tabor.[3]

Christ, My Redeemer . . .

Some days I am a mystery to myself—one moment sitting quietly and contentedly in your presence, the next complaining and fretting over some small annoyance. Open my eyes, Lord, to the gift of suffering, even when my cross feels very heavy, for I know that you never leave me to carry it alone. Through the life and words of Padre

Pio, open my eyes to the way of Calvary, so that I might know the joy of Easter morning. Amen.

Conclude your time of reflection and prayer with one Our Father, one Hail Mary, and one Glory Be.

The Diary of a Soul

The great and constant struggle in the life of
the saint was against the enemies of God and
souls, those demons who sought to capture
his soul.

—Fr. Gabriele Amorth

The life of Padre Pio remains shrouded in mystery; however, we get glimpses of his childhood in his letters to his spiritual directors. There he recounts moments when, as a child, he would play with the Christ Child, always in the presence of Mary. He had never spoken of these experiences, assuming them to be common occurrences. He was too humble to think otherwise. In these moments, we begin to understand how this man, who suffered the Passion of Christ every day of his life for fifty years, still remained so joyful. His was a heart full of love, in constant communion with invisible mysteries. Even as he fought the dark forces of evil, he found consolation in the continuous presence of the Blessed Mother and his Guardian Angel.

In these precious letters to Padre Agostino and Padre Benedetto, there emerges a kind of diary of a soul, revealing a saint in the making. We also find that Padre Pio's suffering began when he was a young child. He would scream in terror whenever his mother turned off the lights at night. Demons would appear, dispersing only when his mother turned the lights back on.

Upon entering the novitiate, Padre Pio's suffering intensified. Demons tormented him constantly, attempting to make him renounce his faith and trying to convince him that the Lord had forsaken him. However, Padre Pio remained steadfast, enduring the trials and offering up his sufferings to the Lord. Padre Pio took up the Cross of Christ and carried it all the way to Calvary. In a letter to Padre Agostino, dated September 20, 1912, Padre Pio speaks of the joy he feels on carrying the Cross of Jesus.

> I am suffering . . . very much. But thanks to our good Jesus, I still feel a little strength. And when aided by Jesus, what is the creature not capable of doing? I don't desire by any means to have my course lightened. . . . Contemplating the cross on His shoulders, I feel more and more fortified, and I exult with holy joy.
>
> However. I feel within me the great need to cry out louder and louder to Jesus with the Doctor of Grace: "Give me what you command and command what you will."[4] Hence, my dear Father, do not allow the idea of my suffering to cast a shadow on your spirit, or to sadden your heart. So let us not weep, my dear Father. We must hide our tears from the one who sends them, from the one who has shed tears himself and continues to shed them every day. Because of man's ingratitude,

he chooses souls, and despite my unworthiness, he
has chosen mine also to help him in the tremendous
task of men's salvation. This is the whole reason why
I desire to suffer more and more without the slightest
consolation. And this consists of all my joys. (*Letters
I*, 342)

Reflect

As we can see, every physical and spiritual trial of Padre
Pio was embraced willingly and joyfully. Trials signify
profound dignity and an exalted destiny. In essence, trials
signify profound dignity because they reveal our capacity
for growth, resilience, and empathy. They challenge us
to rise above difficulties, develop our character, and seek
meaning, all of which underscore our inherent worth and
ability to navigate the complexities of life with grace and
strength. Padre Pio was profoundly touched and humbled,
recognizing the undeniable truth that the Lord desired
his collaboration to fulfill the redemption of humanity.

In Padre Pio's heart, the call from God to sacrifice for
the sake of others became increasingly insistent. Padre
Pio passionately desired to offer his soul for God's glory
and for human ingratitude. He longed to spread acts of
kindness and compassion, fostering unity and healing
divisions. These aspirations were pleasing to God. And
yet, their ultimate realization in his life would come only
through mysterious afflictions of both soul and body.
Reflect on the following words of Padre Pio:

This heart of mine is Yours . . . my Jesus, so take this heart, fill it with Your love and then order me to do whatever You wish.[5]

Christ, My Redeemer . . .

As Padre Pio placed his soul at the foot of the Cross, let us place our souls beside him, and through the Cross, let us journey to the gates of heaven, where we will find you, Our Lord who triumphed over death. Amen.

Conclude your time of reflection and prayer with one Our Father, one Hail Mary, and one Glory Be.

Weekend

The Companion of My Childhood (Consolation)

> One day in 1946 [Padre Pio's father] Z'Orazio fell down a steep flight of stairs in Mary's house. Miraculously he survived. During his convalescence, he complained about his suffering. One day he told his son about his pain and Padre Pio said, "Instead of complaining, thank your guardian angel who put a pillow on every step!"
>
> —Dorothy Gaudiosse, *Mary's House*

If every day was a via dolorosa, a route of suffering through Jerusalem, for Padre Pio, he also knew the consoling presence of the Blessed Mother and the Angels—in particular his Guardian Angel—who often sustained him in the dark moments and strengthened him to keep moving forward, following in the footsteps of the Redeemer. Padre Pio said, "How close to us stands one of the celestial spirits, who from the cradle to the grave never leaves us for an instant."[6]

Throughout his letters, Padre Pio wrote of the great battles he faced in opposing the devil and his demonic hoards, who resisted him and his good works at every step. And yet he also acknowledged the blessing and assistance of a "good Angel"—his Guardian Angel—who fought alongside him, ensuring a positive outcome. In the following letter dated December 13, 1912, Padre Pio expresses his deep gratitude to Padre Agostino for his letters, which he describes as a source of tender consolation.

My very dear Father,

Te Deum laudamus [you, God, we praise]. I have been able at last to read your lines. Your letter, so full of tender consolation, has done good to my afflicted soul. How can I thank you, my beloved Father, for being thus united with my sufferings, even though this has sometimes brought you some consolation? I shall be grateful to you for your care of me and for the sufferings you have shared with me. I am most grateful for all this and hope to repay you a hundredfold when I am close to Jesus. . . .

With the help of the good angel, that wretch has been vanquished this time in his wicked design and your letter has been read.[7] The angel had suggested to me to sprinkle your letters with holy water before opening them. I did this with my last, but can I tell you how enraged the ogre was? He wants to put an end to me at all costs and is using all his diabolical cunning to this end. But he will be crushed. The Angel assures me of this and paradise.

The other night the devil appeared to me in the likeness of one of our Fathers and gave me a very strict order from Father Provincial not to write to you anymore as it is against poverty and a serious obstacle to perfection. I confess my weakness, dear Father, for I wept bitterly, believing this to be a fact. I should never have even faintly suspected this to be one of the ogre's snares if the Angel had not revealed the fraud to me. The companion of my childhood tries to lessen the pains which those impure apostates inflict on me by cradling my soul in a dream of hope.

I am at peace, resigned to everything, and I hope these diabolical tricks will not produce the disastrous effects which frightened me for a while. (*Letters I*, 361)

Reflect

There is a good lesson about our Guardian Angels in this message: No matter what we've done, good or bad, our Guardian Angel never leaves our side. If you feel discouraged, misunderstood, abandoned, or forgotten, know the truth: that you are never truly alone. Ask for the light of truth, and Jesus will shine it into your heart.

What about when you find yourself in trouble and unable to see a way out of the situation? Listen to Padre Pio and call on your Guardian Angel:

Remember that God is inside of us when we are in the state of His grace, and outside of us when we are in grievous sin; but His angel never abandons us. He is our most sincere and trusted friend even when, through our fault, we sadden him with our bad behavior.[8]

Christ, My Redeemer ...

Thank you for entrusting me to the Blessed Mother and to my Guardian Angel. When my circumstances become too heavy to bear, let your words to the Chosen People shine the light of truth upon me: "I am sending an angel before you, to guard you on the way and bring you to the place I have prepared" (Ex 23:20). Jesus, my Redeemer, thank you for the faithful presence of the Angel who guards my way. Amen.

Conclude your time of reflection and prayer with one Our Father, one Hail Mary, and one Glory Be.

Joining Our Hearts to the Heart of Padre Pio

First Week of Lent

Mary, My Solace, My Sweetness, and My Joy

Let us try to penetrate as far as possible with the grace of the Holy Spirit into that marvelous world of the spirit where Padre Pio's heart appears in full harmony with the heart of our Heavenly Mother.

—Most Rev. Paola Carta, "Padre Pio and the Immaculate Heart of Mary"

How Our Lord suffered on the way to Calvary! Weakened and barely able to move, he dragged himself, step by step, as soldiers beat him every time he fell under the Cross. Padre Pio lived this reality every day of his life. He knew the strap of the soldiers; he knew the crown of thorns and the weight of the Cross. Over and over, he walked the road to Calvary. He knew it all because he experienced it all at every Mass he celebrated.

How is it possible that Padre Pio could endure such suffering? Mary! Our Blessed Mother was always at his side, just as she was at the side of Jesus on Calvary. In those moments when the devil came to torture him, Padre Pio would call upon Mary, and she would rush to his side.

Padre Pio never complained about the suffering. He considered it an honor that the Lord chose him to take up his Cross. For Padre Pio, no matter how much he suffered, he sought only to comfort Our Lord. And in his lowest and most discouraged moments, he would think about Mary's visits, and he would find himself full of joy. We read of one such precious visitation in a May 1912 letter to Padre Agostino:

My dear Father,

How often have I confided to this mother the painful anxieties that troubled my heart! And how often has she consoled me? . . . In my greatest sufferings, it seemed to me that I no longer have a mother on this earth but a very compassionate one in Heaven. But many times, when my heart was at peace, I have forgotten all this almost entirely. I have even forgotten my duty of gratitude towards this blessed Heavenly Mother!

Poor dear Mother, how you love me? . . . What great care she took to accompany me to the altar this morning. It seemed to me that she had nothing else to think about except myself as she filled my whole heart with sentiments of holy love. I felt a mysterious fire in my heart which I could not understand. I felt the need to put ice on it, to quench this fire which was consuming me. (*Letters I*, 311)

Reflect

In this letter, Padre Pio told Padre Agostino about all the joy he experienced when Mary was by his side. In those moments, Padre Pio did not talk about his suffering at the consecration or mention how the devil pulled the Chalice from his hands. No, when Mary was with him, he could only think of the joy of her presence.

Mary was always at Padre Pio's side. She and the Child Jesus visited little Francesco Forgione often. At the age of fifteen, when Francesco made the decision to defend Our Lord against the devil, the Lord promised him he would never leave him alone. And he never did! For the fifty years that Padre Pio had the Stigmata, each night when the devil came to beat and torture him, Our Lord and Our Lady never left his side. Mary was at Padre Pio's side just as she was at Jesus's side on the road to Calvary and at the foot of the Cross. She caused Padre Pio's sorrow to turn to joy.

Mary is the greatest intercessor. She brings all our petitions to her Son. Go to your Mother Mary when you are troubled or in need of help; she will always bring your requests to Jesus. Mary is the Virgin most powerful, the Virgin most merciful, the Cause of our Joy, the Comforter of the Afflicted. Always pray to her! Hear the words of Padre Pio:

> Go and keep company with Jesus in His Passion, and with His Sorrowful Mother.[9]

Christ, My Redeemer . . .

On this journey, may our hearts be cleansed of every earthly passion as we humble ourselves and pray. In this way, we will certainly find God, who will give us peace and serenity in this life and eternal beatitude in the next. Amen.

Conclude your time of reflection and prayer with one Our Father, one Hail Mary, and one Glory Be.

Suffering and Abandonment to God

The devil appeared to him under many different forms: as a big black cat, wild and threatening, or as a repulsive animal, in the clear intention to frighten him.

—Fr. Gabriele Amorth

The Lenten journey is about sacrifice. The greatest sacrifice of all is that Christ our Redeemer gave his life so we would be saved. On this Lenten journey we follow Padre Pio who made many sacrifices, but none greater than the one he made for Christ. Padre Pio took up the Cross of Christ in thanksgiving for our Redeemer's suffering.

G. K. Chesterton said, "Every age is converted by the saint who is most unlike it."[10] In this age, Padre Pio stands out as a remarkable figure in the fight against modernism, serving as a living testament to the reality of heaven and hell. Because of his example, we see the necessity of regarding our life on Earth as a pilgrimage toward our divine destination.

During the season of Lent, let us revive our awareness of the spiritual battle we must all fight, each in our own way, just as Padre Pio lived Lent every day in defense of Our Lord. He suffered greatly and loved deeply!

In the following letter dated February 24, 1911, Padre Pio asked Padre Benedetto how he was to observe Lent given his situation. He had already received his invisible Stigmata (September 1910), and it was obvious that his suffering had already begun long before this spiritual milestone. Yet, Padre Pio questioned if he was doing enough!

My very dear Father,

Do not think that my long silence means that I have had less need of your good advice and your exhortations during these days, for in this you would be greatly mistaken. I did not write because I was ill. As regards the spiritual afflictions and battles, I can assure you that they keep pace with my bodily sufferings. When the latter are multiplied the former also increases. I do not know where I shall end up if things go like this.

I thank the Lord, though, that despite the fact that ... I suffer moments of real anguish, I am invariably cheerful, though I must do great violence to myself, and it seems to me that fresh courage is greatly invading my heart. Meanwhile I cast myself trustfully into the arms of Jesus, then let whatever he has decreed take place and he must certainly come to my aid.

I want to ask you a favor. The holy season of Lent is close at hand, and you are well aware of my condition. I should like to know then what exactly you consider to be my obligations during this period. Only in this way will I be able to keep a peaceful conscience. Recommending myself to your prayers with best regards I kiss your hand. (*Letters I*, 243)

Reflect

It is astonishing to me that Padre Pio is so concerned about Lenten sacrifices considering he made sacrifices every day of his life. In the Catholic Church, we are taught to fast and make sacrifices during Lent. Even when we are young, we think about what we will give up. As we mature, our understanding of Lent expands to include not just what we give up, but what we can do to serve others—including the dearly departed. Reflect on these words of Padre Pio:

> Don't draw back, and worse still, don't stop going up the Calvary of life. Jesus will extend His hand to steady you. The thought of the sustaining grace of God and the prize Jesus has reserved for you will be a sweet comfort.[11]

Christ, My Redeemer . . .

On this journey, we keep our eyes fixed on you, O Lord, our guide to the heavenly country, where Padre Pio is also leading us. Whether you wish to guide us to heaven by way of the desert or by the meadow, so long as you are always with us, we will arrive at the possession of a blessed eternity. Amen.

Conclude your time of reflection and prayer with one Our Father, one Hail Mary, and one Glory Be.

Wednesday

A Flame of Intense Love

A thousand years of enjoying human glory is
not worth even an hour spent sweetly com-
muning with Jesus in the Blessed Sacrament.
—Padre Pio

In the following letter from Padre Pio to Padre Benedetto, we listen to excerpts of Padre Pio's description of
"the flame of intense love" that had touched his heart,
an extraordinary experience that had rendered his soul
nearly speechless. He found himself ascending to greater
heights, encompassing a greater compassion for others,
and feeling a surge of trust in God.

My very dear Father . . .

Five months have elapsed since I last gave you
an account of my conscience. Since then, the merciful Lord has helped me powerfully by His grace.
The Lord God has bestowed very great gifts on
my soul. . . . I no sooner begin to pray than my
heart is filled with a fire of love. This fire does not
resemble any fire on this lowly earth. It is a delicate
and very gentle flame which consumes without
causing any pain. It is so sweet and delightful that
it satisfies and satiates my spirit to the point of

insatiability. Dear God, this is a wonderful thing for me, something I will perhaps never understand until I get to heaven.

Far from diminishing the satisfaction of my soul, this desire increases it. . . . The same is to be said of the desire to enjoy continually this intense flame, for the desire is not extinguished by the delight experienced but is rather perfected by this delight. . . . It seems to me God has poured out many graces of compassion for the suffering of others, especially the poor and needy.

The immense pity I experience at the sight of a poor man gives rise deep down in my soul to a most vehement desire to help him. If I were to follow the dictates of my will, I should be driven to strip myself, even of my clothing, to cover him. When I know that a person is afflicted in soul or body, what would I not do to have the Lord relieve him of his suffering? Willingly would I take upon myself all his afflictions to see him saved, and I would even hand over to him the benefits of such sufferings, if the Lord would allow it. (*Letters I*, 517)

Reflect

What would it be like to experience such an intense flame of love? Many believers experience moments when the presence of Jesus is felt more profoundly than others. At times, these sensations may linger, even permeating the days that follow. And yet, as we read this letter of Padre Pio to Padre Benedetto, it is clear this saint had never

encountered such an intense flame of love before. This
newfound experience filled him with overwhelming joy,
almost beyond containment.

Have you ever experienced the compassion of
Christ—a deep ache in your heart for someone struggling
in poverty? Lent presents us with a fresh opportunity to
dig deep in our pockets, to help alleviate the suffering of
others.

I recall my time as a young girl at Our Lady of Guadalupe Grammar School in Brooklyn, where the nuns
introduced us to the "Rice Bowl." At the start of Lent, we
received cards with slots for coins. We filled these cards
throughout Lent, and the funds were sent to missionaries
in China to assist the poor. Ironically, many of us came
from poor families, though we were comparatively better
off than those we wanted to help. Every contribution, no
matter how small, made a difference. Reflect on Padre
Pio's words:

> The merciful Lord has given me the fatherly help of
> his grace. My heart is as if it were invaded by a flame
> of intense love. My soul has become almost speech-
> less. The extraordinary things are becoming more
> sublime. Compassion for the suffering of others.
> Great increase of trust in God. Intentions for prayers.
> (*Letters I*, 517)

Christ, My Redeemer ...

We walk cheerfully along this path to Calvary with sincere and open hearts, and we always maintain a holy joy, for beyond Calvary lies Easter. Amen.

Conclude your time of reflection and prayer with one Our Father, one Hail Mary, and one Glory Be.

Thursday

A Trial of Fire

> In my soul I feel just that terrible pain of loss,
> of God not wanting me—of God not being
> God—of God not existing. I find no words to
> express the depths of the darkness.
>
> —Mother Teresa

Yesterday's flame of intense love contrasts sharply with the "trial of fire" we will read about today. This is not a consoling fire, but represents a dark night for his soul. And what is the cause? Padre Pio saw many individuals turning away from their faith, and he tells us this was causing a spiritual darkness in his soul!

Just two days after Easter, on April 20, 1914, Padre Pio's heart sensed a profound spiritual void, a sense of being forsaken by God. Though it may seem strange to us, for many saints this is a normal part of the journey toward deepening faith and connection with Christ. As we can see from the above quote, Mother Teresa also passed through a dark night of the soul. Let us take a closer look at the struggles that Padre Pio faced on these dark nights, from a letter written to Padre Agostino on April 20, 1914.

My very dear Father.

I do not conceal from you that it afflicts my heart to see so many souls apostatizing from Jesus, . . . many estranged from God solely because they are deprived of the Divine Word. The harvest is great, but the laborers are few. Who is then to reap the harvest in the fields of the Church, when it is almost ripe? Will it be scattered on the ground because of the scarcity of workers? Will it be reaped by Satan's emissaries who are, unfortunately, both numerous and extremely active? Ah, may the most sweet God never allow this to happen. May he be moved to pity for the poverty of men which is becoming extreme. Let us pray for the cause of Holy Church, our most tender Mother; we must consecrate and sacrifice ourselves totally to God for this purpose and meanwhile go on waiting and expecting. . . .

It is deep night for my soul. All hell is turned loose upon it with cavernous roars, with all the evil of its past life and, what is most terrifying, is that my own fantasy and imagination seem determined to conspire against my soul. The beautiful days spent in the shadow of the Lord vanished completely from my mind. The spiritual torment I endure is such that I should be unable to distinguish it from the atrocious pains of the damned in hell. This torment does not last long, nor could it, for if my soul lives through it, this is only by a remarkable favor from God.

As long as we live, we wretched mortals will never be able to penetrate this secret of God's omnipotence. . . . This is a mystery into which it has not been given to me to penetrate. Among the many trials to which the Heavenly Father has subjected me, this is the most severe. It is a trial of fire, but of a fire completely different from our material fire. These two kinds of fire, however, have a property in common which is their capacity to destroy and consume everything opposed to the free achievement of their purpose. (*Letters I*, 522)

Reflect

Padre Pio used the metaphor of the harvest and the scarcity of laborers to convey the urgency of the spiritual crisis in the Church and the need to save souls. Padre Pio acknowledged there was a decline in the people's faith, and he attributed the crisis to the tumultuous events unfolding in Europe during World War I. The unsettling atmosphere of the war instilled fear among the people, leading some to blame the war on God.

Amid these challenges, Padre Pio underwent periods of spiritual darkness. The devil persistently assailed him with doubts. However, Padre Pio recognized that the Lord would never abandon him. He expressed gratitude to the God who sustained him during these trying moments. For him, these dark nights were, in fact, moments of purification. This trial by fire allowed him to shed his old self and made room for the spirit to endure on his behalf:

Zeal for salvation of souls. It is a deep night for my poor soul. It is a mystery into which I have not been allowed to penetrate. (*Letters I*, 522)

Christ, My Redeemer ...

As we follow Padre Pio through this dark night of the soul, let us remember that at the end of this journey is the joy of Easter. Amen.

Conclude your time of reflection and prayer with one Our Father, one Hail Mary, and one Glory Be.

Friday

ᚷake ᚷhis Ꮒeart of ᗰine

Even at a young age [Padre Pio] was called to
a deep, unique relationship with God.

—John Kubasak

Have you ever struggled with the feeling of being unworthy of God's love and care? Even if we have just been to Confession, we may be mindful of all kinds of shortcomings and weaknesses in ourselves. They are part of the human experience. We all have them. We all feel them. Even Padre Pio.

In the following letter to Padre Agostino, dated March 21, 1912, Padre Pio talked about his happiness in the presence of Jesus. He spoke of the overwhelming love and mercy he received daily from Jesus, despite his own sense of unworthiness.

My dear Father . . .

Only God knows what sweetness I experienced yesterday, the feast of Saint Joseph, especially after Mass, so much so that I still feel it. My head and my heart were burning with a fire which did me good. My mouth tasted all the sweetness of the Immaculate Flesh of the Son of God. Oh, at this moment when I still feel almost all of this sweetness, if I could only bury within my heart these consolations, I should certainly be in paradise. How happy Jesus makes me! How sweet is his spirit! But I am confused and can do nothing but weep and repeat:

Jesus, my food! . . . He continues to love me and to draw me closer to himself. He has forgotten my sins, and one would say that he remembers only his own mercy. . . . Jesus asks me almost all the time for love, and my heart rather than my lips, answers him: "O my Jesus, I wish . . ." and then I cannot continue. But in the end, I exclaim: "Yes, Jesus, I love you: at this moment it seems to me that I love you, and I also feel the need to love you more; but, Jesus, I have no more love left in my heart, you know that I have given it all to you. If you want more love, take this heart of mine and fill it with your love, then command me to love, and I shall not refuse. I beg you to do this, I desire it."

The devil in the meantime does not cease to appear to me in his horrible forms and to beat me in the most terrible manner. But praise be the love of Jesus, who repays me for everything by his visits! (*Letters I*, 299)

Reflect

Even when he experienced ongoing attacks from the evil one, Padre Pio was always aware of the loving presence of Jesus, who wanted the Capuchin saint to surrender more and more of his heart to him. This is what the Lord calls all of us to do, to the best of our ability.

How can we do that? What can we derive from these words of Padre Pio? This above letter portrayed a deep, emotional, and spiritual journey marked by love, gratitude, and a profound sense of connection with Jesus. Padre Pio recognized his personal limitations and prayed that the Lord would give him the ability to love him more! And the Lord is always there to do the same for us, and to help us carry our cross. Reflect on Padre Pio's words:

> You must speak to Jesus also with the heart, besides with the lips. Indeed, in certain cases, you must speak to Him only with your heart.[12]

Christ, My Redeemer . . .

As Padre Pio desired the love of the Lord, so too we ask: Jesus, take this heart of mine and fill it with your love, then command me to love, and I shall not refuse. I beg you to do this; I desire it. Amen.

Conclude your time of reflection and prayer with one Our Father, one Hail Mary, and one Glory Be.

Weekend

I See Paradise

Today I was in heaven, in spirit, and I saw its inconceivable beauties and the happiness that awaits us after death. I saw how all creatures give ceaseless praise and glory to God. I saw how great is happiness in God, which spreads to all creatures, making them happy; and then all the glory and praise which springs from this happiness returns to its source; and they enter into the depths of God, contemplating the inner life of God, the Father, the Son, and the Holy Spirit, whom they will never comprehend or fathom.

—St. Maria Faustina Kowalska, *Diary*

In a letter to Padre Agostino on October 14, 1912, Padre Pio explained that the devil wanted him to sever all ties with Padre Agostino, threatening to do unspeakable things to Padre Pio if he refused. But Padre Pio was not afraid: he knew the Lord saw how weak he was, and he would come to his assistance.

My very dear Father . . .

I feel very weak, it is true, but I am not afraid on this account, for will Jesus not see my anguish and the weight that oppresses me? Has he not told us by the mouth of the royal prophet that: 'He knows of what we are made . . . that, as a Father has compassion on his sons, the Lord has pity on those who fear Him?' The Lord then consoles me and causes me to exalt in my weakness.

Again at night when I close my eyes the veil is lifted, and I see paradise open up before me; and then gladdened by this vision I sleep with a smile of sweet beatitude on my lips and a perfectly tranquil countenance, waiting for the little companion of my childhood to come to waken me, so that we may sing together the morning praise to the Beloved of our hearts.

Oh my dear Father, if the knowledge of my state arouses you even in a single thought other than compassion, I beg of you to direct it to my Beloved on my behalf in token of my appreciation and gratitude. I end now because I am extremely tired, particularly as regards to my sight. . . . Pray for your poor disciple. (*Letters I*, 345)

Reflect

When the devil sought to break ties between Padre Pio and Padre Agostino, Padre Pio found solace in the belief that Jesus perceived his distress and the burdens he carried. He trusted in the Lord to console him and strengthen him during his moments of weakness.

Despite these challenges, Padre Pio closed his eyes, and the veil was lifted, revealing only Paradise before him.

Overflowing with joy, he eagerly anticipated the arrival of his Guardian Angel, so they could, together, offer morning praises to the Beloved of their hearts.

Can you think of a time in your life when you felt tormented? How did you find relief from these feelings? Did you go off to bed, close your eyes, and see Paradise? I think this letter tells us something about the faith of Padre Pio and his unconditional love for the Lord. All the suffering, pain, torments, dark nights, and nights of terror he was willing to accept in order to ease the sufferings of Our Lord and Redeemer reveal this.

Reflect on Padre Pio's words:

> Let us always keep before our eyes the fact that here on earth we are on a battlefield and that in paradise we shall receive the crown of victory; that this is a testing-ground, and the prize will be awarded up above; that we are now in a land of exile while our true homeland is Heaven to which we must continually aspire.[13]

Christ, My Redeemer . . .

In those moments when the devil comes to tempt me, Lord, stand with me and give me strength to fight the temptation. Amen.

Conclude your time of reflection and prayer with one Our Father, one Hail Mary, and one Glory Be.

The Invisible Stigmata

Second Week of Lent

The Rosary: Our Lady's Intercession

> The Rosary was Padre Pio's favored prayer. He prayed it many times a day, decade after decade. He had always a rosary wrapped around his hand or arm, as it was a jewel or a shield. He had other rosaries under the pillow and on the nightstand. He called the rosary his "weapon."
>
> —Padre Fernando da Riese

Padre Pio always spoke of the great graces he received from Our Lady, especially in connection with his frequent offering of the Rosary—at least five times each day! During his dark nights and his nights of terror, Mary always came to comfort him. Many mornings, she stood beside him while he celebrated Mass. On these occasions, when the devil came to torment him, Padre Pio would accept his torment with joy, not wanting Our Lady to be upset by the treatment he was receiving.

As he wrote in the following letter to Padre Benedetto, Padre Pio knew he could never repay Our Lady for the kindnesses she had bestowed upon him throughout his life.

My dear Father Provincial,

Urged by the desire to let you have my news I am sending you this letter. I have been much the same except for the fact that the chest pain seems to have become more persistent during the last few days. I am aware of the cause, and I silently adore and kiss the hand of the one who strikes me, knowing only too well that it is He Himself who afflicts me on the one hand and consoles me on the other.

My only regret, dear Father, is that I have no adequate means by which to thank the Blessed Virgin Mary from whose intercession I have undoubtedly received so much strength from the Lord. It has helped me to forebear with sincere resignation the many humiliations to which I am subject day after day. (*Letters I*, 206)

Reflect

Do you pray the Rosary to call on Our Lady when you need to fight those spiritual battles? She is an amazing intercessor. We need the Rosary, which binds us to Our Lady's heart. Satan may seek to undermine its importance, but he will never succeed.

The Rosary is the prayer of those who conquer all adversities. Some are misguided to believe they can navigate life without the aid of the Blessed Mother. Our Lady's aid is second only to the Mass itself in its spiritual and intercessory power. And Our Lady is a never-failing presence at both. In the words of Padre Pio, "How could the Mother of Jesus, who stood at Calvary's foot, offering her Son for our salvation, not be present at the mystical Calvary of the altar?" (*Letters I*, 208).

Let us strive, like countless holy souls before us, to follow this Blessed Mother, to remain ever close to her. Many churches say the Rosary before or after the morning Mass. It is a good habit to get into. Reflect on Padre Pio's words:

> May the Most Holy Virgin, who was the first to practice the gospel perfectly and in all its severity, even before it was proclaimed, spur us on to follow closely in her footsteps.[1]

Christ, My Redeemer ...

On this journey to Calvary, I pray that Our Lady will walk beside us as we pray the Rosary, Padre Pio's favorite prayer. Amen.

Conclude your time of reflection and prayer with one Our Father, one Hail Mary, and one Glory Be.

Tuesday

Enduring a Continual Martyrdom

> Every tribulation whichever comes our way is
> sent to be medicinal, if we will take it as such,
> or may become medicinal, if we will make it
> such, or is better than medicinal, unless we
> forsake it.
>
> —St. Thomas More, *Utopia*

Anyone who has ever struggled to be free of a sense of guilt or doubt will derive comfort from the fact that Padre Pio, too, wrestled with his own sins.

As Padre Pio's illness progressed, a significant decision was made by the Father Provincial, who approached the Congregation for the Religious to obtain a dispensation from the standard nine-month waiting period, hastening Padre Pio's journey towards priesthood—another step closer to his becoming a gifted confessor who would spend much of the rest of his life in the confessional.

However, in this letter we catch a glimpse of young "Fra Pio," or Brother Pio, seeking advice from his spiritual director, Padre Benedetto. As Fra Pio's illness intensified, he found himself grappling with profound doubts about his faith and the state of his conscience. In a letter dated June 20, 1910, the young Capuchin candidly laid bare the turmoil within his soul. The haunting question of whether he adequately confessed all his sins plagued him relentlessly, leaving him in a state of inner turmoil. Despite his fervent prayers, peace eluded him, prompting him to contemplate the necessity of a general confession to attain spiritual clarity.

In this vulnerable moment, Fra Pio turned to Padre Benedetto, seeking solace and guidance in their shared love of Jesus. He implored Padre Benedetto to stand by him, offering support and reassurance as he navigated this profound trial of faith.

> My dear Father,
>
> I send you this with trembling hands and with a sorrowful heart, not only to inform you of my physical state but to let you know my spiritual condition, which seems to me quite deplorable. I refrain from speaking about my health, because the continual ailments which never leave me, rather than lessen my trust in my heavenly mother and in her son Jesus, [hold out to me] a speedy release of the bonds of this wretched body[2] . . .
>
> Listen, my dear Father, I have been troubled continually in conscience on the score of my past life, so badly spent. . . . I am not sure that I confessed all the sins of my past life or confessed them properly. My dear Father, I need some help that will calm the surging waves in my soul, for, believe me, this is the

thought which is killing me, and I cannot make up my mind on this point. I would like to make a general confession, but don't know whether this would be good for me or not. Help me, Father, for the love of our dear Jesus don't abandon me! I am ready to do everything you tell me.

I still feel tempted at times to neglect daily Communion, but up to the present I have always got the better of myself. May all be for the glory of Jesus. How could I live, my dear Father, if I were to fail, even for a single morning, to receive Jesus? . . . In this torment of the heart I feel greater confidence in God and I am so filled with sorrow for my sins that I endure a continual martyrdom. (*Letters I*, 210)

Reflect

As Padre Pio's illness progressed, he yearned to be released from the confines of his physical body (though of course his life would continue more than fifty years!). What troubled him most was not his physical condition, however, but the state of his soul.

How do you view Confession in your life? Is it time for you to make a good Confession? Don't be embarrassed or worry about forgetting what to say. The graces are there for the taking. Remember—all Catholics are obliged to go to Confession at least once a year (*Catechism of the Catholic Church*, 1457). Padre Pio often told his spiritual children that they should never go more than one week without Confession! Reflect on Padre Pio's words:

In our thoughts and in confession, we must not dwell on sins that were previously confessed. Because of our contrition, Jesus forgave them at the tribunal of penitence. It was there that He faced us and our destitution, like a creditor standing before an insolvent debtor. With a gesture of infinite generosity, He tore up and destroyed the promissory notes which we signed with our sins, and which we would certainly not have been able to pay without the help of His Divine clemency.[3]

Christ, My Redeemer . . .

On this road to Calvary, let us call on Padre Pio to pray for us to make a good examination of conscience and confess our sins. Amen.

Conclude your time of reflection and prayer with one Our Father, one Hail Mary, and one Glory Be.

A Cloud Darkens the Horizon of My Soul

Your will be done. Come, Lord Jesus!
—Last words of St. Augustine

In the letters below, Padre Pio's condition continued to deteriorate. He experienced a new pain at the base of his left lung, pain that would become worse as the months went by.

On July 6, 1910, Fra Pio sent a letter to Padre Benedetto, included below. At the same time, Padre Benedetto sent a letter to Fra Pio, informing him that he had obtained the dispensation for his ordination.

My dear Father,

Perhaps Jesus will really have done with me this time. This new pain is more severe than any of the others. It makes me almost powerless to do anything, and at times I can hardly speak. May the hand of our dear Jesus be blessed, the hand which strikes me and allows me without any merit on my part to suffer something for his love in satisfaction for my many sins!

I received your brief letter which brought great comfort to my troubled soul. But, alas, dear Father,

51

every day is not the same with me! A fresh cloud has come to darken the horizon of my soul. The prince of darkness is starting a new war against me. Since he was defeated by my obedience to you—which I confess with certainly no merit on my part—he has started another no less furious battle against me. . . .

My pen is powerless to describe what goes on in my soul at these moments of his concealment. More than ever, when I approach Holy Communion, the malignant enemy makes me feel uncertain as to whether or not I have dismissed temptation. My dear Father, these are moments of most severe struggle and I have to make great efforts to prevent being deprived of so much consolation! What do you feel about this, Father? Is it the devil who stirs up all this, or am I deceived? Please tell me how I should act. (*Letters I*, 211)

Padre Benedetto's letter regarding Pio's ordination:

My dear Fra Pio,

I have obtained the dispensation. About the 10th or 12th of August you can be ordained to the priesthood. God willing. Towards the middle of this month, you must go to Morcone and there prepare yourself by learning the rubrics. I may perhaps have you ordained by the Bishop of Lucera, to whom I shall recommend you for kindly examination. (*Letters I*, 213)

Reflect

Fra Pio complied with the instructions of the Provincial and arrived in Morcone on July 21, 1910; however, his stay was short-lived. On July 22, 1910, he fell violently ill, and Padre Tomasso of Monte Sant'Angelo, who was both the

Novice Master and Vicar of the Friary, and who attended to him during this time, decided that it was best for Pio to return home. He believed this decision aligned with the wishes of the Father Provincial, as his concern was to prevent Fra Pio's condition from worsening.

With only nineteen days until his ordination, Fra Pio's condition grew worse with each passing day. No one could have looked at this desperately ill young monk and imagine that he would one day be one of the most beloved and widely known priest-confessors of the twentieth century! But God was not done with Padre Pio. And he is not done with you, either. Reflect on Padre Pio's words:

> Lord God of my heart, You alone know and see all my troubles. You alone are aware that all my distress springs from my fear of losing You, of offending You, from my fear of not loving You as much as I should love and desire to love You. If You, to whom everything is present and who alone can see the future, know that it is for Your greater glory and for my salvation that I should remain in this state, then let it be so. I don't want to escape from it. Give me the strength to fight and to obtain the prize given to strong souls.[4]

Christ, My Redeemer . . .

Give me the strength to fight and to obtain the prize given to strong souls. Amen.

Conclude your time of reflection and prayer with one Our Father, one Hail Mary, and one Glory Be.

Ꮐhe Ᏼidden Secret

> While Francis was praying in a secluded spot
> and became totally absorbed in God through
> his extreme fervor, Jesus Christ appeared to
> him fastened to the cross. Francis' *soul melted*
> at the sight . . . from that hour, whenever
> Christ's crucifixion came to mind, he could
> scarcely contain his tears and sighs.
>
> —St. Bonaventure, *Life of St. Francis*

On August 10, 1910, Padre Pio was ordained in the Cathedral of Benevento. Twenty-eight days later, he was deep in prayer beneath an elm tree on the grounds of his family's farm in Piana Romana, known as the "Masseria." It was there that he experienced a profound encounter: Jesus and Mary appeared to him, and Jesus bestowed upon him the sacred wounds of Christ, known as the Stigmata.

On the afternoon of September 7, 1910, Padre Pio showed Don Salvatore Pannullo, the parish priest of Pietrelcina, the wounds he had received. Padre Pio expressed his desire to endure suffering in secret, asking for assistance in beseeching Jesus to remove the visible wounds. Together, they prayed fervently, and miraculously the wounds vanished, yet Padre Pio's suffering persisted. Almost a year would pass before Padre Pio mentioned the invisible Stigmata to Padre Benedetto—here is a letter dated October 1, 1910, expressing his suffering without specifying the Stigmata he had recently received.[5]

My dear Father,

My health has been worse than usual for several days and it is precisely this which prevented me from writing sooner: As I am now feeling a little better . . . Our dear Lord, gives me such strength and courage to bear not only the many ailments He sends me, but even the continual temptations which he in fact permits. And which grow more numerous day by day. These temptations make me tremble from head to foot with the fear of offending God.

I hope that in the future, as in the past, I may not fall victim to them. My dear Father, this suffering is too much for me. Recommend me to the Lord that he may be pleased to give me some other trial, even twice the size, in exchange for this one. I must admit, however, that I am happy even in the midst of these afflictions, because almost every day our good Jesus also makes me taste great sweetness.

Dear Father, ask Jesus once more to set me free from the bonds of this mortal body. Write to me, for your councils do me so much good and tell me again what God wants from this ungrateful creature. I pray for you every morning that you may have patience with me a little longer. I have many things to tell you, but can go on no longer. (*Letters I*, 227)

Reflect

Padre Pio confided in Padre Benedetto about the over-whelming burden of his suffering, yet he omitted to mention that it was compounded by the invisible Stigmata he bore. Despite these trials, Padre Pio discovered moments of joy almost daily, expressing gratitude to the compassionate Lord for these glimpses of profound sweetness.

When we encounter the weight of our crosses, do we turn to the Lord and seek his assistance? Do we perceive our crosses as gifts from the Lord, offering glimpses of profound sweetness? Or do we view them solely as burdens to bear alone? Do we ever ask, "Lord, why have you sent me this cross?" instead of simply pleading, "Lord, help me carry this cross"? Reflect on Padre Pio's words:

> Follow the Divine Master up the steep slope of Calvary, loaded with our cross, and when it pleases him to place us on the cross . . . let us thank him and consider ourselves lucky to be honored in this way, aware that to be on the cross with Jesus is infinitely more perfect than merely contemplating [Him] on the Cross.[6]

Christ, My Redeemer . . .

As we journey to Calvary with Padre Pio, let us carry our own crosses with greater courage and joy. Amen.

Conclude your time of reflection and prayer with one Our Father, one Hail Mary, and one Glory Be.

Friday

My Heart Throbs before the Blessed Sacrament

If you truly love Me, you will love Me even in
darkness. Embrace the Cross . . . be certain
that while you are satisfying your desire of
suffering you are satisfying my heart. . . .
—Jesus to St. Gemma Galgani

While Padre Pio was preparing to take his final vows, he
became gravely ill. The decision was made to ordain him
immediately, though he had not reached the legal age
for ordination, and on August 10, 1910, Padre Pio was
ordained in the Cathedral of Benevento. Since Padre Pio
was so ill, he remained in his hometown of Pietrelcina.
He celebrated his first Mass in Pietrelcina on August
14, 1910.

In an excerpt of a letter to Padre Benedetto dated September 8, 1911, a penitent Padre Pio, still in Pietrelcina,
finally told his spiritual director of the physical manifes-
tation of the Stigmata, which had first transpired over a
year before and which he had suffered (in invisible form)
all that time.

My dear Father.

Yesterday evening something happened to me which I can neither explain nor understand. In the center of the palms of my hands, a red patch appeared, about the size of a cent and accompanied by acute pain. The pain was much more acute in the left hand, and it still persists. I also feel some pain in the soles of my feet.

This phenomenon has been repeated several times for almost a year now, but . . . do not be disturbed by the fact that this is the first time I have mentioned it, for I was invariably overcome by abominable shame. If you only knew what it costs me to tell you about it now! . . . I can only say that when I am close to Jesus in the Blessed Sacrament, my heart throbs so violently that it seems to me at times that it must burst out of my chest. Sometimes at the altar, my whole body burns in an indescribable manner. My face in particular seems to go on fire. I have no idea, dear Father, what these signs mean. (*Letters I*, 264)

Reflect

On September 7, 1910, while praying under the elm tree while grazing sheep at Piana Romana, Padre Pio received the Stigmata. He prayed that the visible Stigmata would be taken away, and for eight years, his Stigmata remained invisible. Padre Pio chose to bear an invisible burden, untouchable, and beyond comprehension, known only to God. Padre Pio treasured this suffering, always wishing to keep it to himself. The more he suffered, the more he pleased the Lord because it demonstrated his willingness to suffer—that is, to take up his cross—in thanksgiving for Christ bearing the Cross for our salvation.

Padre Pio said, "In this life Jesus does not ask you to carry the heavy cross with Him, but a small piece of His cross, a piece that consists of human suffering."[7] Many of us bear these small pieces of the cross every day of our lives. When someone is ill, or someone dies, when life just becomes too unbearable, these are the crosses in our lives.

The Lord doesn't want us to carry these crosses alone! The Lord wants us to call on him. When you find yourself unable to bear the pain of your cross, offer your suffering up for the souls in purgatory or for the poor or the sick, so that through your suffering, others may receive joy. By offering up our crosses and our human suffering to the Lord, our pain is redeemed with a deeper purpose. Reflect on Padre Pio's words:

> Kneel down and render the tribute of your presence and devotion to Jesus in the Blessed Sacrament. Confide all your needs to him, along with those of others. Speak to him with filial abandonment, give free rein to your heart, and give him complete freedom to work in you as he thinks best.[8]

Christ, My Redeemer . . .

Comfort us in all our afflictions. Watch over us always with your grace, and show us the safe path that leads to eternal salvation. Help us to trust you always to lead us nearer to your Divine Heart, and make us more worthy of Paradise. Amen.

Conclude your time of reflection and prayer with one Our Father, one Hail Mary, and one Glory Be.

Weekend

Devotion to Your Guardian Angel

Beside each believer stands an angel as protector and shepherd, leading him to life.
—St. Basil the Great, quoted in the *Catechism of the Catholic Church*, 336

In Padre Pio's letters, the name Annita frequently appears. Initially known only by that name, she was later identified as Annita Rodote, also known as Sister Margherita. Her letters to Padre Pio, found in Letters III, were preserved in the archives of her convent.

Annita spent years seeking entry into a convent. Several years before she was received into the Sisters of the Holy Spirit (on March 23, 1920), Padre Pio asked his friend and spiritual director Padre Agostino to check on Annita, concerned about the state of her soul. Padre Agostino replied to Padre Pio on July 10, 1915.

My beloved son in Christ,

You asked me my opinion about that other soul (Annita), and you asked me to examine her as regards the interior locutions and her manner of prayer. With regard to the locutions, she replied that she seems to hear every now and then the voice of a confessor, as it were, urging her onwards towards good and towards divine love. She experiences these locutions sometime during prayer and sometimes apart from prayer, in the church, at home and in the street. She is afraid there may be some trick here on the part of the enemy. . . . I advised her to reply always. "Jesus, if it is you who speak to me, let me see the effects of your words in me in the form of the holy virtues!"

As regards prayer, she tells me that, up to the present, she has applied herself almost exclusively to vocal prayers, always with the help of a book. I advised her to begin to practice mental prayer a little and I showed her briefly how to go about it.

What do you think, now, of her future state? Will she become a nun? . . . We must pray to Jesus instinctively to remove the obstacles which stand in her way. (*Letters I*, 680)

Five days later, Padre Pio wrote these words to Annita about the importance of being devoted to her Guardian Angel:

My daughter of Jesus,

May your good Guardian Angel always watch over you; may he be your guide on the rugged path of life. May he always keep you in the grace of Jesus and sustain you with his hands so that you may not stumble on a stone. May he protect you under his wings from all the snares of the world, the devil and the flesh.

Have great devotion, Annita, to this good Angel; how consoling it is to know that near us is the spirit who, from the cradle to the tomb, does not leave us even for an instant, not even when we dare to sin. And this heavenly spirit guides and protects us like a friend, a brother. . . .

Always keep him present in your mind's eye. Often remember the presence of this angel; thank him, pray to him, always keep him good company. Open up yourself to him and confide your suffering to him. Have constant fear of offending the purity of his gaze. Know this and keep it well imprinted on your mind; he is so delicate, so sensitive. Turn to him in times of supreme anxiety, and you will experience his beneficial help.[9]

Reflect

Padre Pio's words offer a profound understanding of the significance of Guardian Angels in our lives. As he emphasized, they accompany us from birth to death, guiding and protecting us every step of the way. Reflect on Padre Pio's words:

When Jesus was alone, feeling abandoned, and in agony, God the Father sent an angel to strengthen him. (*Letters I*, 683)

Christ, My Redeemer . . .

Send our Guardian Angels ahead of us on this journey to prepare a safe passage for us! Amen.

Conclude your time of reflection and prayer with one Our Father, one Hail Mary, and one Glory Be.

Demons All Around Me

Third Week of Lent

I Am Greatly Indebted to Our Lady

> God the Father gathered all the waters together and called them the seas or *maria*. He gathered all his grace together and called it Mary or Maria . . . This immense treasury is none other than Mary whom the saints call the "treasury of the Lord." From her fullness all men are made rich.
> —St. Louis Marie de Montfort, "Treatise on True Devotion to the Blessed Virgin"

Padre Pio's deep love for the Madonna was evident in every aspect of his life, from his constant prayers to his tender gestures of devotion. She was his steady companion; his unwavering faith in her intercession transcended mere sentimentality, rooted in deep and unwavering faith; her role in the salvation of souls brought him comfort and strength.

Padre Pio always had a picture in his cell of the Madonna. Whether pausing before meals, retiring for rest, or returning wearily from the confessional, he would cast his eyes upon her with profound gratitude. This ritual persisted until his final moments, as he beheld his beloved Madonna with immense tenderness before closing his eyes in death. Her name was on his lips as he departed this world.

Padre Pio's profound love for the Madonna permeated every facet of his life; in his letter dated June 2, 1911, Padre Pio tells Padre Benedetto of his gratitude to Mother Mary for driving away the temptations of the enemy.

My dear Father. . . .

Our common enemy continues to make war on me, and up to the present has shown no sign of admitting defeat. He . . . presents to my mind the painful picture of my life and, worse still, tries to lead me to thoughts of despair. But I am greatly indebted to our Mother Mary for driving away these temptations of the enemy. Will you too, please, thank this good mother for these exceptional graces which she obtains from me at every moment, and meanwhile please suggest to me some new ways by which I can in all things, please this Blessed Mother?

The greatest sign of love you can show me will be precisely this, that you too thank Our Blessed Lady for me. What makes life more burdensome and tedious for me at present is especially the chest pains. The doctor has told me: 'I can do nothing for you.' This statement does not sadden me by any means; rather do I feel a great desire to abandon myself with greater trust to the Divine Mercy and to place my hope in God alone. (*Letters I*, 253)

Reflect

Padre Pio's devotion to the Blessed Mother was profound and unwavering, deeply rooted in his spiritual journey. For Padre Pio, Mary was not only a figure of reverence but also a compassionate and powerful advocate. Padre Pio entrusted his worries and anxieties to her maternal care, finding comfort in her presence.

In one instance, Padre Pio vividly recounted how she seemed to accompany him to the altar. He experienced a profound, mysterious fire in his heart, a spiritual fervor that he attributed to her intercession. Padre Pio's devotion to Mary serves as a powerful example, inspiring others to deepen their own relationship with the Mother of God. Reflect on Padre Pio's words:

> Let us endeavor . . . to follow this blessed Mother, to walk always close to her, not following any other path that leads to life, except the one trod by our Mother.[1]

Christ, My Redeemer . . .

May Mary be the star which shines on our path, and may she show us the safe way to reach your Heavenly Father. May she be like an anchor to which we must be more closely attached in times of trial. Amen.

Conclude your time of reflection and prayer with one Our Father, one Hail Mary, and one Glory Be.

Tuesday

Jesus, Grant Me a Brief Respite

God is faithful, and he will not let you be
tempted beyond your strength, but with the
temptation will also provide the way of escape,
that you may be able to endure it.

—1 Corinthians 10:13

Padre Pio understood that he had been selected by God
to participate in Christ's redemptive mission, a collaboration that could only be fulfilled through the embrace of
the Cross. For him, the Cross illuminated every step of
his arduous journey, serving as an unending wellspring
of strength, generosity, faithfulness, and perseverance. At
times, despite not actively contemplating it, Padre Pio's
soul ignited with a fervent longing to fully possess Jesus.

In these moments, his soul vividly communicated to
the Lord a vision of his future life as nothing but a model
of suffering, rejoicing in his calling to participate in the
salvation of souls. Constantly assailed by temptations and
fears of failure, at times, Padre Pio lost faith in himself, but
he was always able to pull back in those final moments of

doubt. Much of this was possible because of the comforting words of two fine priests—Padre Agostino and Padre Benedetto—as we find in this letter to the latter, dated October 22, 1910.

> My very dear Father,
>
> Who will set me free from the miseries in which I am placed? The temptations especially pursue me more relentlessly than ever. They are a source of great suffering . . . in view of my great fear of offending God from one moment to the next. . . . It is true that I have been strong up to the present and by God's grace have not yielded to the enemies' wiles, but who knows what may happen to me in the future? I should indeed be glad if Jesus would grant me a brief respite. But may his will be done in my regard!
>
> Even from far away do not fail to invoke maledictions on this common enemy of ours so that he may leave me in peace. I ask you in charity to pray to the Lord for me just as I have done and will continue to do for you, . . . that he may keep me from evil. (*Letters I*, 231)

Padre Benedetto's consoling reply to Padre Pio a week later reminds Padre Pio that temptation is a sign of divine predilection.

> My dear Fra Pio,
>
> It consoles me to hear that the storms are increasing because this is a sign that God's Kingdom is being established within you. Temptations are the sure sign of divine favor[2] and the fact that you fear them is the

clearest proof that you do not yield to them. Keep cheerful then and do not be discouraged. . . . "God is faithful, and he will not let you be tempted beyond your strength . . ." Even Saint Paul was distressed and asked to be set free from the harsh trials of the flesh: he too was afraid he would give in, but he received the assurance that the help of grace would suffice for him. (*Letters I*, 231)

Reflect

These letters revolve around finding comfort and strength in the face of trials and temptations by trusting in God's love and protection. They emphasize that challenges and storms in life are signs of God's kingdom being established within oneself and that temptations, far from being feared, should be seen as indications of divine favor. In Padre Benedetto's letter, he encouraged Padre Pio to maintain cheerfulness and resilience, even in the midst of adversity, by believing in God's faithfulness and the assurance of his grace. The letter underscored the importance of acknowledging God's goodness and care, emphasizing that he is always concerned for our well-being and will protect us against all adversaries. Reflect on Padre Pio's words:

In all the events of life, you must recognize the Divine will. Adore and bless it, especially in the things which are the hardest for you.[3]

Christ, My Redeemer ...

I pray to have the faith of Padre Pio in all things. Amen.

Conclude your time of reflection and prayer with one Our Father, one Hail Mary, and one Glory Be.

Wednesday

Fix Your Eyes on the Humanity of Jesus

> As they were looking on, so we too gaze on his wounds as he hangs. We see his blood as he dies. . . . He bows his head, as if to kiss you. His heart is made bare open, as it were, in love to you. . . . His whole body is displayed for your redemption. Ponder how great these things are. Let all this be rightly weighed in your mind: as he was once fixed to the cross in every part of his body for you, so he may now be fixed in every part of your soul.
>
> —St. Augustine, *De Genesi ad litteram*

As time passes, Padre Pio's heart becomes increasingly attuned to the call of God to sacrificial offering for the sake of others. His soul, fervently desiring to sacrifice itself for God's glory and to express gratitude through reparation, longs for the spread of salvific action throughout the world, illuminating minds and warming hearts like daylight. These aspirations are pleasing to God, and in time Padre Pio comes to recognize that the ultimate fulfillment of this plan—his participation in the Passion—will come through mysterious afflictions of his soul and body, culminating in the Stigmata. Padre Pio fully comprehends its profound beauty and dedicates himself entirely to delighting, comforting, and pleasing Jesus in his sufferings.

In his letter dated November 18, 1912, Padre Pio tells Padre Agostino he is speaking to him not by word of mouth but by his heart. . . .

My dear Father.

By this letter I am coming to speak to you not by word of mouth but by my heart. My lips are sealed, but I am able to speak all the same. The one who is always by my side has come at last to rout the enemy so that I can write you these few lines. But I am very weak. The enemy hardly ever leaves me alone, and he beats me continually. He is trying to poison my life with his infernal snares. . . . He hints that I should tell you about the good visits, as these, he says, are the only ones which can please and edify you. Dear God, what a martyrdom is the temptation to vainglory. It seems to have no importance, yet we must be convinced of the very opposite. One needs to pass through this fire to understand its extreme intensity. To overcome it, one needs to keep one's eyes fixed on the humanity of Jesus. Jesus, his beloved Mother, the little Angel, and the others continue to encourage me . . . [and] to have such a tender Father by one's side in the battle is sweet and consoling.

When the Archpriest became aware of the attacks of these impure apostates with reference to your letters, he advised me to go to him on receipt of your next letter so as to open it in his presence. This I did on receiving your last. But when we opened it we found it completely covered with ink stains! . . . I cannot believe you would have sent it to me like that, aware as you are of the weakness of my sight. At first the writing seemed illegible to us, but after we had placed the letter on the crucifix it became a little clearer, although we can only read it with great difficulty. This letter has been kept carefully. (*Letters I*, 354)

Reflect

Padre Pio recognized that love and embracing the Cross were integral to his journey. Choosing the path of the Cross, Padre Pio was firmly convinced that his life would be defined by martyrdom. Yet, he found joy in the knowledge that he was summoned to participate in the salvation of souls through the profound experience of suffering, deriving its value from a genuine sharing in the Cross of Jesus. While many may overlook this aspect of his life, it was foundational to his spirituality. Without the reality of the Cross, Padre Pio's holiness would be incomplete. Reflect on the following words of Padre Pio:

"How often," Jesus said to me just now, "would you have abandoned me, my son, if I had not crucified you . . . ?"[4]

Christ, My Redeemer . . .

Help me to be patient in enduring tribulations, illness, and pain, for the love of God and for the conversion of poor sinners. Amen.

Conclude your time of reflection and prayer with one Our Father, one Hail Mary, and one Glory Be.

Thursday

A Mortal Agony Invades My Wretched Soul

> The great and constant struggle of Padre
> Pio's life was with those enemies of God and
> human souls, the devils who tried to capture
> his soul.
>
> —Fr. Gabriele Amorth

Padre Pio expressed his love for the Cross unequivocally: "I love the cross, the cross alone." His entire life and heart were consecrated to the Cross, eternally carried on Jesus's shoulders, and to sharing in Christ's suffering on the road to Golgotha, offering solace without seeking any comfort for himself.

In his letter dated October 30, 1914, Padre Pio tells Padre Agostino he is writing this letter because it is what Jesus wants.

> My very dear Father, . . .
>
> Those wicked spirits, dear Father, are making every effort to destroy me. They wanted to beat me at all costs. They seem to take advantage precisely of my bodily weakness, to vent their rage upon me more

fully, to see if in this state, they cannot snatch from my breast the faith and fortitude that come to me from the Father of all light.

At certain moments I see myself actually on the brink of the precipice and then it seems to me that the tide of the battle is about to turn in favor of those scoundrels. I feel myself trembling all over. A mortal agony invades my wretched soul and overflows into my poor body. My limbs appear to me to be paralyzed. Then it seems to me as if my life had stopped, as if it were suspended.

This is a sad and mournful spectacle: only one who undergoes this trial can imagine it. . . . I confess, my dear Father, that in all these battles, I am so weak that it seems I must succumb from one moment to the next. I feel certain, nevertheless that according to my expectation and hope, I shall never be confounded and that Jesus Christ, as is invariably the case, will now be glorified in my soul and in my body which will suffer no damage whatsoever. . . . My entire person is consecrated to Jesus, to whom I feel united by a two-fold bond, as a Christian and as a priest. Precisely on this account do I tremble at the mere thought that this double bond might be momentarily loosened.

Is it possible for this bond to be broken; or, what is worse, could it possibly have been broken unknown to me? I feel certain that this is not the case, with a certainty that can only be equaled by my certainty of God's existence. My dear Father, I am aware that this is talk of a foolish person but let me be foolish. It is

my love for Jesus that has brought me to this point.
(*Letters I*, 557)

Reflect

When Jesus desires to reveal his love to Padre Pio, he allows him to intimately experience the wounds, thorns, and agony of his Passion. When he wishes to bring Padre Pio joy, he fills his heart with a fervent spirit and speaks of delights. But when God seeks delight, he beckons Padre Pio to offer his body.

Reflect on the following words of Padre Pio:

Humility and purity are the wings which carry us to God and make us almost divine.[5]

Christ, My Redeemer . . .

On this journey, make us humble as you made Padre Pio humble. Amen.

Conclude your time of reflection and prayer with one Our Father, one Hail Mary, and one Glory Be.

Friday

Dark Nights of Terror

> If I ever become a saint—I will surely be one
> of darkness. I will continually be absent from
> Heaven—to (light) the light of those in dark-
> ness on earth.
>
> —Mother Teresa

During World War I, Padre Pio was frequently summoned to Naples for medical examinations by the Italian Army. Each time he was given convalescent leave due to his poor health. The war had taken its toll on Padre Pio, and the increased spiritual combat caused his dark nights to explode into nights of terror, with wild beasts constantly circling him. At such times, he would often write to his spiritual directors; as always, these letters spoke of both physical and spiritual illness—and were his only consolation in these times of terror.

On January 3, 1917, Padre Agostino wrote regarding Padre Pio's upcoming convalescence; an infection in his lungs had caused the medical examiner to order a six-month leave for the Capuchin priest. Padre Agostino wrote:

My beloved son in Jesus Christ,

May Jesus be ever and everywhere blessed! . . . I thank him with all my heart for letting me have your news at last. I wrote five or six times to Pietrelcina, but in vain. Now your own letter has arrived, and may the Lord be thanked. Although I expected this grace for you from the Divine Mercy, I was anxious and uneasy. Let us now thank Jesus for the grace he has granted us as He pleased. You are happy and so am I. Let us hope that peace will return to the world and that Jesus will spare you a further cross after six months. However, may His holy will always be done!

As regards your spiritual state, please don't let yourself be completely cast down. Bear in mind all the time the assurances of authority and let that be sufficient. Unfortunately, you are suffering, and you must suffer, but isn't it for Jesus, with Jesus and in Jesus? Don't be afraid, then. This most tender God is with you, and that is enough for you. If Jesus prolongs your exile, don't complain, make known the divine goodness to many souls; spend yourself as best you can for the spread of Jesus' Kingdom in souls. (*Letters I*, 952)

Padre Pio's reply to Padre Agostino on January 6, 1917, was brief.

My very dear Father,

May Jesus always live in your heart and in all the souls who belong to him. I have just received your letter here, and I can't tell you the relief it brought me in my rather dejected state of soul. May Jesus reward you abundantly. Forgive me, Father, if I am brief because

I haven't the strength to go on. The trial I have passed
through in the last few days has exhausted my strength.
With great warmth I embrace and kiss you, asking you
on my knees for your fatherly blessing, while I remain
entirely yours. (*Letters I*, 954)

In his letter dated January 6, 1917, Padre Pio's letter
to Padre Benedetto is full of darkness.

> My very dear Father,
>   May Jesus assist you always in all the trials of
> life. . . . The mere thought of what I went through
> during those days terrifies me and makes me shudder.
> Spiritual combats are always on the increase. Thick
> darkness pervades my soul and I behold nothing
> but darkness, always darkness. I see nothing except
> wild beasts prowling around me and threatening to
> make me their prey. I hear nothing but the howling of
> these beasts which makes me die with fright at every
> moment. Alas, my dear Father, when will this state
> end? (*Letters I*, 956)

World War I went on for another year and a half with the
fighting coming to an end on November 4, 1918.

Reflect

Padre Pio found himself engulfed in terror amid those
dark nights. As his spiritual battles intensified, with thick
darkness enveloping his soul, he was left with nothing but
a bleak, unending void. Reflect on the following words of
Padre Pio:

Let us always keep before our eyes the fact that here on earth we are on a battlefield and that in paradise we shall receive the crown of victory; that this is a testing-ground and the prize will be awarded up above; that we are now in a land of exile while our true home-land is Heaven to which we must continually aspire.[6]

Christ, My Redeemer . . .

When I am feeling the dark terrors of the night, may Padre Pio lead me on a path of light, and into the presence of Our Lord, the light of the world! Amen.

Conclude your time of reflection and prayer with one Our Father, one Hail Mary, and one Glory Be.

Weekend

The Guardian Angel and the Letters

For he will command his angels concerning you,
to guard you in all your ways.
On their hands they will bear you up,
so that you will not dash your foot against a
stone.

—Psalm 91:11

In his letter dated November 5, 1912, Padre Pio tells Padre Agostino that there is a new war being waged against him—thwarting Padre Pio's efforts to maintain communication with his spiritual directors.

My dear Father,

This second letter; by God's permission, met with the same fate as the previous one. I am certain that by this time Padre Evangelista has informed you about the new phase of the war waged on me by those impure apostates. . . . I cannot tell you the way these scoundrels beat me. On Saturday it seemed to me that they intended to put an end to me, and I did not know what saint to invoke. I turned to my Angel and after he had kept me waiting a while, there he was hovering close to me, singing hymns to the divine majesty in his angelic voice. There followed one of the unusual scenes; I rebuked him bitterly for having kept me waiting so long when I had not failed to call him to my assistance. To punish him, I did not want to look him in the face, I wanted to get away, to escape from him. But he, poor creature, caught up with me almost in tears and held me until I raised my eyes to his face and found him all upset. Then: "I am always close to you, my beloved young man," he said. "I am always hovering around you with the affection aroused by my gratitude to the Beloved of your heart. This affection of mine will never end, not even when you die. I know that your generous heart beats all the time for the One we both love; you would cross every mountain and every desert in search of him, to see him again, to embrace him. . . . You must wait a little longer. For the present he can give you nothing like the ray of a star, the perfume of a flower, the strains of a harp, the caress of the wind! But do not cease to ask him incessantly for this, because his supreme delight is to have you with him. And although he cannot yet satisfy you, since Providence wills that you remain in exile a little longer, he will gratify you in the end at least in part". . . . Poor little Angel! He is too good. Will he succeed in making me appreciate the serious duty of gratitude? (*Letters I*, 350)

In his reply, Padre Agostino offered consoling advice to his spiritual son, reminding him that the whole of hell's army is subject to God's permission.

My beloved Son in Jesus Christ,

I am pleased to hear of the new phase in the war which our wicked enemy wages on you continually. Do not fear him, for he will always be utterly defeated. It does not matter if he comes accompanied by all forces, because the whole of hell's army is subject to God's permission. Guard holy humility towards the divine will at all times, for the proud tempter trembles at the humility of God's children. Always call on your Guardian Angel in every temptation, for he is always near you. What can the tempter do to a soul that places all its trust in the Good God. The battle will end, and the soul will enjoy an immortal victory. (*Letters I*, 353)

Reflect

Our Guardian Angel is always close to us. We should never fail to call on him to pray beside us, especially in moments of trial. Reflect on the following words of Padre Pio:

May your good Guardian Angel always watch over you and be your guide on the rough path of life. May he always keep you in the grace of Jesus and hold you up with his hands so that you may not hurt your foot on a stone.[7]

Christ, My Redeemer . . .

On this journey, let us pray that our Guardian Angels will gather us under their wings and protect us from all the deceits of the world, the devil, and the flesh. Amen.

Conclude your time of reflection and prayer with one Our Father, one Hail Mary, and one Glory Be.

Mystical Touches

Fourth Week of Lent

Monday

Who Is This Who Is Near Me?

Am I not here, I, who am your Mother? Are
you not under my shadow and protection?
Am I not the source of your joy? Are you not
in the hollow of my mantle, in the crossing of
my arms? Do you need anything more? Let
nothing else worry you or disturb you.
—Our Lady of Guadalupe to St. Juan Diego

Throughout Church history, the Blessed Mother and other
saints and angels have appeared as messengers of mercy
and grace to those most in need of it—and yet the first
words of that message are very often, "Do not be afraid."
This supernatural brush, heaven touching earth for a brief
moment, is intended for consolation—and yet it is alto-
gether sobering for those who feel unworthy of the honor.
This was as true for Padre Pio as it was for Juan Diego.

In Padre Pio's letter to Padre Agostino, dated May 6,
1913, we understand that Our Lady showers Padre Pio
with exceptional attention, offering solace as he struggles
between longing for death and clinging to life.

My dear Father.

What have I done to deserve such delicacy? . . . This most tender mother in her great mercy, wisdom and goodness, has been pleased to punish me in a most exalted manner by pouring so many and such great graces into my heart. When I am in her presence and in that of Jesus, I am compelled to exclaim: "Where am I? Where do I find myself? Who is near me?" I am all aflame, although there is no fire. I feel myself held fast and bound to the sun by means of this Mother; without seeing the chains which bind me so tightly. A thousand flames consume me; I feel I am constantly dying, yet I am still alive.

At certain moments the fire . . . is so intense that I make every effort to draw away, to go in search of water, icy water into which to plunge. But alas, my dear Father, I realize at once how unhappy I am . . . that I am not free: I feel the invisible chains binding me tightly to Jesus and his beloved Mother; and it is at these moments, more often than not, that I flare up. I feel the blood coursing in my heart and then to my head, and I am tempted to cry out to them, to call the Son Cruel and the Mother Tyrant.

But dear God! I am no longer master of myself, and I am aware that this is madness. Then, when I succeed in controlling myself and reflect on my life . . . I have the strength to protest that I would not exchange it at any price for many other lives in this world. I'd like to fly off to invite all creatures to love Jesus and Mary. . . . An immense gladness fills my whole heart and makes me blissful and content. I suffer and I want to suffer more;

I feel I am being consumed. . . . I long for death for no
other reason than to be united by indissoluble bonds to
the heavenly Bridegroom. (*Letters I*, 403).

Reflect

In this letter, Padre Pio reflected deeply on the undeserved
abundance of grace bestowed upon him by the Blessed Mother,
despite his own failings and unworthiness. He marveled at the
spiritual experiences he encountered in the presence of Jesus
and Mary, describing a sensation of being engulfed in flames of
divine love and bound tightly to them, even though he could
not physically perceive the chains that bound him.

The intensity of this spiritual fire caused him to
momentarily recoil. In moments of weakness, he was
tempted to rebel against this divine embrace. And yet,
despite the challenges and suffering inherent in his spiritual journey, Padre Pio found profound joy and content-
ment in his union with Jesus and Mary.

Reflect on the following words of Padre Pio:

Always stay close to this Heavenly Mother, because she
is the sea to be crossed to reach the shores of Eternal
Splendor.[1]

Christ, My Redeemer . . .

On this journey, let me learn how to love and suffer more
so that I might find this thing that I am seeking. Amen.

*Conclude your time of reflection and prayer with one Our
Father, one Hail Mary, and one Glory Be.*

Tuesday

A Touch or Embrace of Union

When we are expecting only suffering, the least joy surprises us: Suffering itself becomes the greatest joy when we seek it as a precious treasure.

—St. Thérèse of Lisieux

Padre Pio described a deeply spiritual experience he felt during Mass. His heart and Jesus's heart were united in such profound intimacy, they seemed to merge into one. This "fusion of hearts" produced such overwhelming joy that Padre Pio shed tears of happiness. In this letter dated April 18, 1912, he described this encounter with the "Divine Prisoner":

My Dear Father,

Praise be to Jesus. I am delighted to be able to converse a little with you in this letter. . . . I confine myself to relating what happened to me last Tuesday. What a burning fire I felt in my heart that day, lit by a friendly hand, by a divinely jealous hand. . . .

There were things which cannot be translated into human language without losing their deep and heavenly meaning. The heart of Jesus and my own—allow me to use the expression—were fused. No longer were two hearts beating but only one. My own heart had disappeared as a drop of water is lost in the ocean. Jesus was its paradise, its King. My joy was so intense and deep that I could bear no more, and tears of happiness poured down my cheeks.

Yes, dear Father, man cannot understand that when paradise is poured into a heart, this afflicted, exiled weak and mortal heart cannot bear it without weeping. I repeat that it was the joy that filled my heart which caused me to weep for so long. This visit, believe me, restored me completely. Praise be to the Divine Prisoner! (*Letters I*, 307)

Reflect

The concept of the Fusion of Hearts, as experienced by Padre Pio, is a mystical phenomenon characterized by a profound spiritual union between an individual and God. Mystical touches refer to the supernatural imprinting of delightful feelings by God through a spiritual contact at the deepest level of the soul. Distinguished by their varying degrees of intensity, deeper touches are often described as "substantial" because they seem to occur between two distinct substances—namely, God and the soul.

While some interpretations may suggest that these experiences take place solely within the mind or faculties of the soul, Padre Pio's own account challenges this notion. He explicitly stated that his heart and the heart of Jesus were fused together, transcending the physical and conceptual boundaries of separate entities. This fusion signifies a profound and intimate spiritual connection, where the individual becomes united with the divine in a way that surpasses mere intellectual or emotional comprehension and produces sublime happiness. Reflect on Padre Pio's words:

> The heart of Jesus and my own, allow me to use the expression, were fused. No longer were two hearts beating but only one.[2]

Christ, My Redeemer . . .

Unite my heart with yours, that I might be completely united to you. Flood my soul with a sense of your presence, as near as my next breath. Wash my soul clean, that I might come to your altar at Easter shining like the dawn of your ascent into heaven. Amen.

Conclude your time of reflection and prayer with one Our Father, one Hail Mary, and one Glory Be.

Wednesday

I Am Crucified by Love

> He will provide the way and the means, such
> as you could never have imagined. Leave it
> all to Him, let go of yourself, lose yourself on
> the Cross, and you will find yourself entirely.
> —St. Catherine of Siena

As Padre Pio progressed on the spiritual path, grace continually acted directly on his soul, manifesting also in his body and senses. Prayer became increasingly passive, revealing the vastness of God's greatness and humanity's frailty. Various mystical phenomena, such as transports of love, wounds of love, and spiritual raptures, occurred with varying frequency and intensity, increasing as he advanced in life. He describes these experiences to Padre Benedetto in this letter dated March 18, 1915:

My very dear Father,

May I be allowed to express myself freely, at least to you: I am crucified by love! I can no longer go on. This is too delicate a food for one accustomed to coarse fare, and it is for this reason that it continually causes me extreme spiritual indigestion. My poor soul cries out in acute pain and love at the same time. My wretched soul cannot adapt to this new manner of the

Lord's dealing with it. Thus, the kiss and the touch, which I would describe as substantial, that this most loving Heavenly Father imprints on my soul, still cause me extreme suffering. . . .

I implore you to tell me what you think about this. Having to attend to the necessities of life, such as eating, drinking, sleeping, etc., is so burdensome to me, [like] the pains which our martyrs must have suffered in their supreme trial. Do not think, Father, that there is any exaggeration in this comparison. . . . I feel the ground giving way beneath my feet. May the Lord assist me and free me from this great torment. May He behave towards me and treat me as I ought to be treated. (*Letters I*, 610)

Reflect

Love and suffering were intrinsic components of Padre Pio's spiritual journey, part of a divine plan not fully revealed to him at the outset. He experienced alternating spiritual consolations and inexplicable joys alongside excruciating sufferings, akin to the torments of hell. Along the path, new favors and graces emerged, drawing his soul closer to a transformative union with God. Love and suffering coexisted, deepening his interior connection with God and enhancing his service to others.

After his soul underwent purification through the night of senses, it entered a mysterious dark night of the spirit. The purification of his faculties grew more painful, leaving his soul feeling lost and isolated in despair.

Throughout his journey, Padre Pio experienced both sweet consolations and agonizing sufferings, grappling with the anguish of his human nature. Yet, he remained restrained, in perfect harmony with God's will and fully submissive to the mysterious plan of divine Providence.

Reflect on the words of Padre Pio:

> Let us, therefore, love to quench our thirst at this fountain of living water and go forward all the time along the way of divine love. But let us also be convinced that our souls will never be satisfied here below. In fact, it would be disastrous for us if, at a certain stage of our journey, we were to feel satisfied, for it would be a sign that we thought we had reached our goal, and in this we would be deceived.[3]

Christ, My Redeemer . . .

As we advance on this journey, may we proceed happily and full of hope in our Homeland, where we will stay eternally. May we firmly believe that God calls us to himself and is following us along this path towards him. He will never permit anything to happen to us that is not for our greater good. He knows who we are, and he will hold out his paternal hand to us during difficulties, so that nothing prevents us from running to him swiftly. To enjoy this grace, we must have complete trust in him. Amen!

Conclude your time of reflection and prayer with one Our Father, one Hail Mary, and one Glory Be.

Thursday

A Fusion of Hearts

> The night . . . is a most painful trial but a very
> lovable one.
>
> —Padre Benedetto

In moments of grief or sorrow, our suffering increases
when we allow ourselves to imagine that God has abandoned us. This is a temptation that can assault even the
most spiritually advanced—such as Padre Pio. And yet,
the Lord—who in his earthly journey also experienced
this spiritual isolation—continually draws us into that
intimate encounter if we open our hearts to him—just as
Padre Pio did.

In his letter dated March 8, 1916, we can sense Padre
Pio's spiritual anguish. His dread of justified abandonment consumes him. He experiences fleeting moments of
divine embrace, initially fraught with fear, then engulfed
in ecstasy. Hell besieges him as his human weakness
tempts him to relinquish any hope of divine union. He
yearns for a reprieve from self-condemnation, even in
what may be his final moments.

My very dear Father.

I keep my eyes fixed on the east, in the night which surrounds me, to discover that miraculous star which guided our forebears to the Grotto of Bethlehem. But I strain my eyes in vain to see that luminary rise in the heavens. The more I fix my gaze, the dimmer my sight becomes; the greater my effort, the more ardent my search, the deeper the darkness which envelops me. I am alone by day and by night, and no ray of light comes through to enlighten me. Not a cooling drop comes to mitigate the flame which devours me continually without ever consuming me. . . . I was seized with the greatest fear, and by degrees this fear became a heavenly rapture. It seemed to me that I was no longer in the state of a traveler, and I cannot tell you whether or not at that moment I was still aware of being in this body of mine. Only God knows this, and I am unable to tell you anything further to give you a better idea of this event.

But dear God, who could ever have imagined what was to happen to me shortly afterwards! Hell was turned loose upon me. . . . I was thrust back into a darker prison than before, where I am at the present and where nothing reigns but everlasting horror. . . . I see the impossibility of this union for me. I see within my soul qualities which are quite in contradiction to this union.

Dear Father, I am unable to go on. I am unable to hold the pen, shaken with sobs which rob me of speech. How am I to act so as not to offend the Lord? Have patience with me on this account and do me the favor of putting it down in writing for me. (*Letters I*, 841)

In his March 9, 1916, response to Padre Pio, Padre Benedetto talked about the phenomenon Padre Pio encountered and explained that this touch or embrace of unity was a gift from the Lord to console him and fortify him for the tempest that loomed ahead.

> My dear son.
>
> The night in which you are immersed and bewildered is a most painful trial, but it is very lovable because of the fruit it produces in the soul. It is intended to extinguish human understanding so that divine understanding may take over, so that, stripped of the common way of thinking and the ordinary exercises of the mental faculties, you may ascend to what is purely supernatural and heavenly. . . . By this obscurity God intends to prepare you for the extremely spiritual vision of His beauty and greatness. (*Letters I*, 848)

Reflect

Padre Pio grappled with his inability to fully experience the Divine and his dread of justified abandonment. Initially fraught with apprehension, then overwhelmed with ecstasy, he couldn't discern whether the experience was internal or external. Reflect on Padre Pio's words:

> Once did I feel in the deepest recesses of my spirit something so delicate that I do not know how to explain it. (*Letters I*, 842)

Christ, My Redeemer ...

May we feel your presence and loving touch in our souls.
Amen.

*Conclude your time of reflection and prayer with one Our
Father, one Hail Mary, and one Glory Be.*

Friday

A Living Breath

The Spirit of God has made me, and the breath
of the Almighty gives me life.

—Job 33:4

Europe was still engulfed in World War I. On Corpus
Christi 1918, Padre Pio experienced a sudden shaking
and tremor of terror. Amid this upheaval, a divine calm
descended upon his soul, stirring within him a desire to
offer himself as a victim to God, in accordance with the
pope's intention for the cessation of hostilities. In his letter
dated July 27, 1918, Padre Pio tells Padre Benedetto about
an unusual event that took place at Mass.

My very dear father.

I see myself obliged to go on living in the midst of
this total abandonment, when it is desirable to die at
every moment as a relief from the agonizing life I am
living. Alas! My God. My God. Why have you forsaken
me? I can utter no other cry from the profound bitterness of my heart where I behold myself condemned.
Useless were my modest efforts to hold out against this
ferocious heat; I am bereft of life; I can no longer hold
out. It is urgent that I should live by you and in you
and with you, or else I shall die. Oh, life and death! My

hour is terrifying, and I do not know, my dear Father, how I can go any further, and who knows how much longer this dreadful hour will last.

Tell Jesus not to be a tyrant to me any longer; He makes me seek Him exceedingly, and since I seek Him among the elect without finding Him, there arises this awful temptation to seek Him among the enemy ranks. This is a dreadful temptation against which to fight. It seems to scatter and overturn and demolish everything that the half-dead soul can put together in order to cultivate the thread of hope which makes me hope against hope itself.

I find myself obliged to live in this state without the slightest respite and with increasing difficulty which has made my situation unspeakably distressing ever since the feast of the holy Apostles. Here is what happened to me on that day. During my Mass in the morning, I was touched by a living breath. . . . I felt completely shaken, filled with extreme terror, and I almost passed away. This was followed by a state of total calm such as I had never experienced before. Something . . . I felt touching me in the deepest recesses of my soul. . . .

While this was taking place, I had time to offer myself entirely to the Lord for the same intention which the Holy Father had when he recommended to the whole Church to offer prayers and sacrifices. I had hardly finished doing so when I felt myself falling into this most harsh prison and heard the loud clang of the prison door as it closed behind me. Cruel shackles seemed to close in on me and bind me tightly, and I felt I was about to die. Since that moment I have felt myself in hell without even an instant of respite. (*Letters I*, 841)

In his responding letter, Padre Benedetto encouraged Padre Pio to see that he was not alone in his torment.

> My dear Puccio, . . .
>
> The "why have you forsaken me?" can receive no other answer than the death decreed on Cavalry which no lament can change, because if life did not die, death would live, death which was also so displeasing to the Heart which loved so much the life of those who were dead. . . . And what was the meaning of the interior touch on the morning of Corpus Christi? It meant that God adhered to your soul and shook it, infusing into it a stream of life, like an elixir to sustain you when you were placed on the gallows. That is the whole fact of the matter. (*Letters I*, 848)

Reflect

Let's contemplate for a moment on the profound encounter that Padre Pio had with this Living Breath within his soul! Then let us turn our hearts toward God and ask him to breathe on us as well. Reflect on Padre Pio's words:

> Stay with me, Lord, for as poor as my soul is, I want it to be a place of consolation for You.[4]

Christ, My Redeemer . . .

Breathe on me, Lord. Come close to us and breathe on us. Amen.

Conclude your time of reflection and prayer with one Our Father, one Hail Mary, and one Glory Be.

My Guardian Angel Gave Me a Sermon

Our Guardian Angels are our most faithful friends, because they are with us day and night, always and everywhere. We ought often to invoke them.

—St. John Vianney

Padre Pio humbly accepted his role as a chosen instrument of Jesus; he expressed a willingness to endure suffering for his sake, even finding joy in being considered as Jesus's "plaything." This expression signifies Padre Pio's humility and willingness to be used by Jesus in whatever way he saw fit, regardless of Pio's own perceived worthiness.

In the following letter, dated January 18, 1913, Padre Pio recounts to Padre Agostino a specific incident where he confronted demons with a scornful attitude and was defended—and exhorted—by his Guardian Angel.

My dear Father.

Praise be to Jesus. I should like to tell you a great many things, but where am I to start? At the moment

I am greatly weighed down by physical suffering and I'm almost tired before I begin. But Jesus will help.

It seems to me that our Lord's words, which seemed so obscure before, are beginning to have clear meaning for me: "Love is recognized in suffering, and this you will feel acutely in your soul, and even more acutely in your body." To the trial of spiritual fears and trembling with an occasional spice of desolation, Jesus is . . . making use of those ugly wretches for this purpose.

Listen to what I had to endure a few evenings ago from those impure apostates. The night was already well advanced when they began their attack with devilish din . . . then they appeared to me in the most abominable forms. But thank heaven I scolded them soundly and treated them as they deserve. Then, when they saw all their efforts going up in smoke, they hurled themselves on me, threw me to the ground and proceeded to beat me very severely. Throwing pillows, books and chairs around the room with desperate shrieks and most obscene language. . . .

I complained to my Guardian Angel, and after giving me a little sermon, he said, "Thank Jesus, who is treating you as one chosen to follow him closely up to the steep ascent of Calvary; soul confided by Jesus to my care, I behold with joy and deep emotion this behavior of Jesus towards you. Do you perhaps think I should be happy if I did not see you ill-treated like this? I, who in holy charity greatly desire your good, rejoice more and more to see you in this state. Jesus permits me these assaults of the devil because he in his compassion makes you dear to him, and he wants you to resemble himself in the torments he endured in the desert, in the garden, and on the Cross. Defend yourself, always reject and despise the devil's evil insinuations . . . do not be distressed, beloved of my heart, for I am close to you."

What condescension, dear Father!! What have I ever done to deserve such exquisite kindliness on the part of my Angel? But I do not worry about this by any means. Isn't the Lord free to bestow his graces on whomsoever he wills and in the way that pleases him? (*Letters I*, 1169)

Reflect

Despite the distress caused by these assaults, Padre Pio found comfort in the belief that Jesus permitted these trials out of compassion, aiming to draw him nearer to himself. His Guardian Angel reassured him of Jesus's care, urging him to reject temptation and rely on divine strength. Humbly accepting his role as a chosen instrument of Jesus, Padre Pio trusted in Jesus's love and sovereignty, even finding joy in being his instrument.

Let us remember that Jesus allows trials in our lives to bring us closer to him. Will you accept these trials, and help Our Lord carry his Cross to Calvary? Reflect on the words of Padre Pio:

"By repeated blows of the saving chisel and by diligent cleansing, I am accustomed to prepare the stones that are to form part of the eternal edifice." Jesus repeats these words to me each time he makes me a present of a new cross.[5]

Christ, My Redeemer . . .

On this journey, as in all things, let us call on our Guardian Angel to pray for us and protect us on this and all our journeys in this life. Amen.

Conclude your time of reflection and prayer with one Our Father, one Hail Mary, and one Glory Be.

Padre Pio's Stigmata

Fifth Week of Lent

Monday

Longing for My Heavenly Homeland

The atrocious sufferings of his soul are
reflected in his body.

—Padre Agostino

In his letter dated May 9, 1915, Padre Pio told Padre Agostino that he was in a profound spiritual struggle. He was deeply aware of the presence of both divine grace and spiritual warfare. He felt besieged by the trials of life and the assaults of Satan, finding his only solace in the protection and guidance of his heavenly Mother, in whose intercession he trusted for his ultimate victory.

My very dear Father.

May Jesus and Mary enable you to grow more and more in charity and make you increasingly worthy of the heavenly homeland. The enemies are continually rising up, Father, against the ship of my spirit, and they cry out in unison: "Let us knock him down, let us crush him, since he is weak and cannot hold out much longer."

Alas, my dear Father, who will set me free from these roaring lions all ready to devour me? You say, only too well, that while the Lord is testing us by His crosses and suffering, He always leaves in our hearts a glimmer of light by which we continue to have great trust in him and to see his immense goodness. This light, in fact, has never grown less, but you have to agree that it is precisely this light which causes the soul greater pain than can be humanly conceived. It shows up the divine goodness as something the soul can enjoy by loving possession, something it can only long for from afar with painful yearnings to possess it. This light makes the soul yearn for God. The source of all good, and more often than not, the pain of its desire is revealed by abundant tears.

Do not imagine that the body has no point in these atrocious sufferings experienced by my soul. No, it participates in a very surprising way that is quite unknown to the children of suffering.

You can now imagine, Father, the extent of my suffering. You already understand from what I have said that the light itself which comes from above becomes, for my soul, a most painful torment. Add to this the war waged by Satan and the entire life of the soul becomes unendurable.

We must have no illusions about the enemy who is exceedingly strong, if we do not intend to surrender. In the light infused by God the soul understands the great danger to which it is exposed if it is not continually on its guard. The idea of losing all by a possible fall makes my poor soul tremble like a reed in the wind.

I told you a while ago that the strength of Satan who fights against me is something terrible, but may

God be praised, for He has placed the cause of my salvation and the ultimate victory in the hands of our heavenly Mother. Protected and guided by so tender a Mother I will continue to fight as long as God wills, full of confidence in this Mother and certain that I will never succumb.

How far away is the hope of victory, Father, viewed from this land of exile? How close and certain it is, on the other hand, when viewed from God's house, beneath the protection of this most holy Mother? . . .

Elsewhere I told you in the Lord what was acceptable to God and what you were to do for salvation of your neighbors, without ever considering it's sufficient. To this I now add that you must be careful and always keep a vigilant watch over yourself, especially as regards the abominable vice of vainglory, which is the woodworm, the consuming moth of devout souls. You must watch out for this vice all the more so since it is easier for it to enter the soul and make headway unobserved and hence is much less easily recognized. We must always be on our guard, and we can never fight too hard against this tireless enemy who is always there on the doorstep of every action. (*Letters I*, 643)

Reflect

Despite the distance and uncertainty of his current situation, Padre Pio found hope in the certainty of victory when viewed from the perspective of God's house. He acknowledged his own weaknesses and the need for constant vigilance against the insidious vice of vainglory.

Through obedience and trust in God's goodness, he found peace and strove to fulfill his duties while seeking spiritual growth and salvation.

Reflect on the words of Padre Pio:

> In my greatest sufferings, it seems to me that I no longer have a mother on this earth, but a very compassionate one in Heaven.[1]

Christ, My Redeemer . . .

On this journey, let us grow spiritually, as Padre Pio did, so that we too can find a room in the house of the Lord. Amen.

Conclude your time of reflection and prayer with one Our Father, one Hail Mary, and one Glory Be.

Tuesday

A Bed of Sharp and Cruel Thorns

Desire to see God, be fearful of losing Him,
and find joy in everything that can lead to
Him. If you act in this way, you will always
live in great peace.

—St. Teresa of Avila

In this letter dated June 4, 1918, Padre Pio told Padre
Benedetto of a bleak prison shrouded in impenetrable
darkness. The tempest raged, and the enemy's relent-
less assault sought to overwhelm him in the storm. God
seemed elusive; the very notion of a divine presence had
faded, leaving him adrift in the abyss. He found himself
incapable of love, unable to grasp onto anything substantial. He questioned where the guiding light had gone. He
felt he was slipping away. He found himself left in the
depths of despair and deprived of love's warmth.

My very dear Father,

I postponed writing to you until now for the simple reason that I didn't want to burden you excessively,
aware as I am of the load you already have to bear.

But I have come to the point where I can no longer go on. . . . I feel the Lord's hand weighing heavily on me. I feel he is punishing me, with all his might, and like a leaf carried off by the wind I am cast off and then pursued by him.

Alas! I can no longer bear it! I can no longer endure the weight of his justice. I feel myself crushed by His mighty hand. Tears are my daily bread: I toss and turn; I seek him but do not find him unless in the fury of his justice.

My dear Father, I can well say with the Prophet: I am out in the open sea and the tempest has submerged me; I have cried out and struggled in vain. My throat has become hoarse but to no avail. Fear and trembling have come upon me, and darkness has covered me on all sides. I am stretched out on my bed of pain panting in my search for my God. But where am I to find Him? From my bed of suffering and my prison of expiation I try in vain to come forth to life. . . .

I am looking for God but where am I to find him? Even the idea of a Lord and God has vanished; of a master, creator, love and life. He has dispelled everything and I, alas, I'm lost in the thickest darkness, while I return in vain to disconnected memories of a lost love and am no longer capable of loving. Oh my great Good, where are you to be found?

. . . I have no further control over my reason or my heart. There is no longer any life in me and with this strangling death in my soul I have no grip on life anymore. No news of any kind is capable of dispelling this mortal sleep of mine. I cling, or rather, it seems to me that I cling, and I don't know how, to those prudent aids, you have given me up to the present. I bow my head and endeavor still to bow it willingly beneath all the blows of the divine justice rightly enraged with me, but nothing is capable of reviving lasting life within me, nothing can raise up my mortally wounded spirit. I become drowsy, then I faint. At times my spirit is jolted and roused by the demands of its lost treasure. . . . I am alone with my fiery character, alone with my internal and external vexation, alone with my natural corruption, alone in combat with the enemy.

My supreme Good. Where are you? My God. My God! I can no longer say anything else to you, why have you forsaken me? (*Letters I*, 1148)

Reflect

It is the cry of Christ himself from the Cross: "My God, my God, why have you forsaken me?" (Mt 27:46). Padre Pio was bewildered, unable to make sense of his situation. He had lost control of both his reason and his emotions. He felt as though life was drained from him.

Reflect on Padre Pio's words:

My Supreme Good, I will endeavor to find a resting-place in my unbearable affliction on this bed of sharp and cruel thorns. (*Letters I*, 1150)

Christ, My Redeemer ...

Let us safely pass from this night of torment. Amen.

Conclude your time of reflection and prayer with one Our Father, one Hail Mary, and one Glory Be.

Wednesday

An Interior Martyrdom

> We always find that those who walked closest to Christ were those who had to bear the greatest trials.
>
> —St. Teresa of Avila

As Padre Pio traversed the path toward Calvary, Satan persisted in sowing seeds of fear and doubt. Padre Pio exclaimed, "Where can I encounter God? Where might this weary heart find solace?" (*Letters I*, 1153). Despite ceaseless seeking, God eluded him; knocking at the door of the Divine yet receiving no answer, in his despair he queried, "May I in the end come to love you with the love you demand?" (*Letters I*, 1153).

Padre Pio pondered his fate at the conclusion of this frantic, agonizing quest, unaware that this path would lead him to his final martyrdom in life—the Stigmata. In this letter dated June 19, 1918, Padre Pio reluctantly revealed to Padre Benedetto his state of being in interior martyrdom.

My very dear Father.

I call together all the scattered faculties of my soul at this moment, in order to put down on this paper, if possible, the entire interior martyrdom which my soul experiences in being deprived of its Supreme Good. But dear God! None of these faculties respond to the appeal. How true, dear God, unfortunately, is what you say by the mouth of your Prophet: "If the Lord does not build the house, in vain do its builders labor." Oh, my dear Father, my wandering spirit eludes my search, it vanishes in a disheartening diffusion, similar to what it feels and experiences when it makes the least attempt to approach the mere idea of its God. . . .

O heaven! O life! What vision are you withdrawing from me? Don't you know that without you I am deprived of my very existence and can no longer go on without dying? My dear Father, it is only by bridling my soul and shutting it up in silence. Only by hiding from all creatures that I keep myself, to some extent, from puzzling my head over my interior martyrdom.

But the abominable book is always open. Creatures, like the Creator, are always present and therefore the sight of what they are doing inevitably provokes shrill cries of overwhelming need of God and the vociferation of continual sleepless longing for Him. . . . O my dear Father, don't abandon this soul that is so ungrateful to his God; don't cast off this blind man who has trampled on holy joys so as to feed on nothing but what was unclean! Dear God! . . . I seek Him, my dear Father, from the deep precipice over which I see myself falling headlong, and if at times I seem to find Him, He then eludes me, and I can no longer find or grasp him. Then my weary arms drop dejectedly and in the futile agitation of my soul in search of its

Supreme Good what agony, what a cruel martyrdom, what infernal torment the poor thing endures. . . .

My dear Father, when will this dreadful torture come to an end? It seems to me that all the beauty of grace has been torn out of my soul. . . . Forgive my hard heartedness, my dear Father, by which I feel constrained and which I cannot conceal. Continue to bless me and don't stop helping me. You may be sure that I pray constantly for you and offer myself all the time, to God. With deep respect, I kiss your hand. (*Letters I*, 1153)

Reflect

Consider how Padre Pio reacted to this interior martyrdom. His soul sensed abandonment, confronted by horror. He perceived himself plummeting into an abyss, and as he reached for God, the divine seemed to slip away, eluding his grasp. His weary arms drooped in despair as the fruitless quest for his Supreme Good became agony, a cruel martyrdom, an infernal torment. Reflect on the words of Padre Pio:

Fear not, because God is with you.[2]

Christ, My Redeemer . . .

On this journey with Padre Pio, let us offer our little crosses for those who feel abandoned by God. Amen.

Conclude your time of reflection and prayer with one Our Father, one Hail Mary, and one Glory Be.

Thursday

The Seraph's Assault

How gently and lovingly you wake in my heart, where in secret you dwell alone; And in your sweet breathing, filled with good and glory, how tenderly You swell my heart with love.

—St. John of the Cross, *The Living Flame of Love*

On August 5, 1918, Padre Pio experienced a mystical occurrence known as the transverberation of the heart. This event, sometimes called a seraph's assault, is considered a sanctifying grace.

According to the teachings of Saint John of the Cross, during transverberation, a soul inflamed with love for God is deliberately pierced by a Seraph, igniting the soul with divine fire and filling it with delightful sweetness. For Padre Pio, this experience served as a prelude to the extraordinary event of the Stigmata, which occurred just over a month later, on September 20. In our letter today, dated August 21, 1918, Padre Pio explained to Padre Benedetto what happened on the night of the transverberation.

My very dear Father,

May Jesus be always with you and repay you in a hundredfold for the good you are endeavoring to bring to my soul! . . . O Way, Truth and Life, give me what my soul needs before I am submerged in the vast and abysmal ocean which invites and attracts me inexorably in order to swallow me up!

My dear Father, my strength is inadequate to endure such frightful agony, such awful torture. This is the third day that I am obliged to remain powerless in bed. . . . The attack is fearful on every side, in every way, touching every substance, every point, every purpose, every turn. Every virtue is exposed to danger. . . .

I am quite unable to convey to you what occurred during this period of utter torment. While I was hearing the boy's confession on the evening of the 5th, I was suddenly terrorized by the sight of a celestial person who . . . had in his hands a sort of weapon, like a very long, sharp-pointed steel blade, which seemed to emit fire. At the very instant that I saw all this, I saw that person hurl the weapon into my soul with all his might. I cried out with difficulty and felt I was dying. I asked the boy to leave because I felt ill and no longer had the strength to continue.

This agony lasted uninterruptedly until the morning of the 7th. I cannot tell you how much I suffered during this period of anguish. Even my entrails were torn and ruptured by the weapon, and nothing was spared. From that day on I have been mortally wounded. I feel in the depths of my soul a wound that is always open which causes me continual agony. (*Letters I*, 1182)

Reflect

Consider the profound inner turmoil and suffering experienced by Padre Pio during this heavenly assault. He found himself utterly powerless, unable to act in the face of his agony. The pain inflicted upon him by the celestial being was overwhelming; the wound in his soul felt eternal, rendering him immobile for two days in anguish. Despite his prayers, he found no respite from his torment, leading him to question whether this suffering was a divine punishment. This piercing is a little difficult to understand. Padre Pio is not the only saint to have received this. St. Teresa of Avila said her piercing profoundly shaped the course of her life. Every day, she committed herself fully to serving Jesus Christ, whom she saw as the perfect embodiment of God's love. She frequently spoke and wrote about how Jesus's suffering redeemed a broken world and how the pain allowed by God could serve meaningful purposes in people's lives.

For Padre Pio, the piercing was the same, but the purpose was different. His piercing was to purge his soul and prepare him for the Stigmata. You might wonder why this was necessary. What could be greater than sharing the wounds of Christ? In fact, those wounds are sacred. They made Padre Pio one with Christ. His body, as perfect and pure as it was, still needed to be purged to accept the wounds of Christ. Reflect on the words of Padre Pio:

> I feel in the depths of my soul a wound that is always open, and which causes me continual agony. (*Letters I*, 1182)

Christ, My Redeemer . . .

You are my breath and my life. Today, trembling, I elevate you in a mystery of love. In your mercy, let my heart unite with yours, so that in both joy and pain my offering pleases you. Amen.

Conclude your time of reflection and prayer with one Our Father, one Hail Mary, and one Glory Be.

Friday

The Stigmata

He feels the blood pouring out of his heart like
a fountain of water.

—Padre Benedetto

The Spanish Influenza, which infected hundreds of millions of people worldwide between 1918 and 1920, was one of the deadliest pandemics in the history of the world. Padre Pio himself was infected by the disease not long after receiving the Stigmata, as we read in this letter to Padre Benedetto dated October 17, 1918.[3]

> I am writing to you after a very long silence and you will surely forgive me, aware as you are that it was not due to negligence or indifference but to absolute powerlessness. I have been in bed with Spanish influenza which is causing a number of deaths here also. I would have greatly desired the Lord to call me to himself, but he has restored me to this miserable existence and to the combat of this world.

Padre Pio continued writing his letter and making suggestions, but he did not find the strength to tell Padre Benedetto about his Stigmata until October 22, 1918.

My very dear Father,

May Jesus, the Sun of justice, always shine on your soul, enveloped in the mysterious darkness of the trial which He Himself has willed, and directly! What can I tell you in answer to your question regarding my crucifixion?

On the morning of the 20th of last month in the choir, after I had celebrated mass, I yielded to a drowsiness similar to a sweet sleep. All the internal and external senses and even the very faculties of my soul were immersed in indescribable stillness. Absolute silence surrounded and invaded me. I was suddenly filled with great peace and abandonment which effaced everything else and caused the lull in the turmoil. All this happened in a flash.

While this was taking place I saw before me a mysterious person similar to the one I had seen on the evening of August 5th. The only difference was that his hands and feet and side were dripping blood. The sight terrified me and what I felt at the moment is indescribable. I thought I should die and really should have died if the Lord had not intervened and strengthened my heart which was about to burst out of my chest.

The vision disappeared and I became aware that my hands, feet and side were dripping blood. Imagine the agony I experienced and continue to experience almost every day. The heart wound bleeds continually especially from Thursday evening until Saturday. Dear Father, I am dying of pain because of the wounds and the resulting embarrassment I feel deep in my soul. I am afraid I shall bleed to death if the Lord does not hear my heartfelt supplication to relieve me of this condition. Will Jesus, who is so good, grant me this grace? Will he at least free me from the embarrassment caused by these outward signs? I will raise my voice and will not stop imploring Him in His mercy, that He takes away, not the wound or the pain, which is impossible since I wish to be inebriated with pain, but these outward signs which cause me such embarrassment and unbearable humiliation. . . .

My God! Your punishment is just and your judgment right, but grant me your mercy. Lord, with your prophet I shall continue to repeat: "O Lord do not rebuke me in your anger; do not punish me in your rage." (*Letters I*, 1217)

Reflect

In his letters, Padre Pio vividly articulated the depths of his profound desolation, a state he endured with poignant intensity. With persistent entreaties, he fervently sought an end to his spiritual exile, yearning for relief from the trials that besieged him. Amid this arduous journey, he exemplified heroic humility, a remarkable virtue nurtured by the radiant illumination and tender solace that flooded his soul. Reflect on Padre Pio's words:

Don't be afraid, then, that iniquity will triumph over virtue. Iniquity will crush itself and justice will triumph. (*Letters I*, 1218)

Christ, My Redeemer . . .

Let us then exclaim in the peace of exceedingly bitter suffering: May his will be done. Amen.

Conclude your time of reflection and prayer with one Our Father, one Hail Mary, and one Glory Be.

Three Angelic Creatures

> I have great reverence for Saint Michael the
> Archangel; he had no example to follow in
> doing the will of God, and yet he fulfilled
> God's will faithfully.
>
> —St. Faustina Kowalska

In this letter dated July 21, 1913, Padre Pio told Padre
Benedetto about a vision that left him trembling.

My very dear Father,

On Sunday morning after I had celebrated Mass,
here is what happened to me: My soul was suddenly
carried away by a force stronger than itself into a very
large room illuminated by a very bright light. On a
high throne studded with jewels was seated a lady of
rare beauty. This was the most holy Virgin who held
in her arms the Child of majestic men, His face more
resplendent and luminous than the sun. All around
them was a great multitude of very beautiful Angels.

At the end of this large room there were two small
beds, in each of which was a person who, to judge by
appearances, must have been in great suffering. One
of them was suffering so much as to seem on the point
of bidding farewell to this life.

Before the throne on which the Virgin was seated there was another person, completely absorbed in contemplation, who was the personification of happiness. The Child came down from the Virgin's arms, and, followed by His mother and the Angels, approached the person rapt in prayer. He threw his arms around that person, clasped her to His breast, kissed her an infinite number of times and bestowed on her innumerable other caresses. The Virgin and the Angels did likewise.

Then He went towards the beds of the two sick persons. To one of these, who was sitting up in bed, the Child addressed just a few words of comfort, rather coldly and unceremoniously. At the other sick person who lay at full length in the bed and had greater need of comfort, He did not deign even to glance, and as if He hated even to punish her, He ordered the angels to beat her. These did not hesitate to carry out His orders. They approached the sick person, one of them took her hand and the others began to punch and kick and slap her.

This scene seemed very cruel. But what a strange and wonderful thing! The poor creature did not complain, but in a very weak voice exclaimed: "O most gracious Jesus, have mercy on me while the time for mercy still lasts. Do not condemn me, most sweet Jesus, when you come to judge me, for I should not be able to love you anymore. O most compassionate Jesus, if your severe justice intends to condemn me, I appeal to your most loving mercy."

The Child turned to me and said: "Learn how one should love." I understood nothing. This site made me tremble like a reed exposed to a violent wind, for I expected this soul to be rejected by Jesus. But alas how different from the reality is sensual man's estimation of spiritual things!

Wretched me! For many years I have attended the school of suffering without learning anything. May the infinite mercy of our God be eternally blessed for his great goodness and patience in bearing with me. . . .

All three of these angelic creatures were in God's grace; all were adorned with merits, though not equal in measure, for the third was more fully adorned by merit than the second and the second more than the first. Since I could not understand why the Lord treated in such different ways these dear spouses of His, He was pleased to come to the aid of this wretched creature and by a clear and explicit interior locution he began to say to me: "The first was a soul still weak and in need of caresses, otherwise she would have turned her back on Him; the second soul was less weak, and to keep her in His service she still needed some little sign of affection; the third was a beloved spouse of His, because, in spite of the way He afflicted her, she remained constant in her service and faithful in love." (*Letters I*, 436)

Reflect

In a divine vision, Jesus interacted with three suffering individuals: one received close comfort, another endured indifferent treatment with humility, and the third remained steadfast despite severe affliction. Jesus explained that their responses reflected their spiritual states: one needed affection, another encouragement, and the third was deeply devoted despite affliction.

In this letter, Padre Pio was speaking of divine mercy, love in adversity, and the mystery of God's ways, revealing the beauty of souls devoted to God, and the power of divine grace. Reflect on the words of Padre Pio:

> Your tears were collected by the angels and were placed in a golden chalice, and you will find them when you present yourself before God.[4]

Christ, My Redeemer . . .

May the angel of God, my guardian, to whom the goodness of the Heavenly Father entrusts me, enlighten, protect, and guide me now and forever. Amen.

Conclude your time of reflection and prayer with one Our Father, one Hail Mary, and one Glory Be.

Carry the Cross toward Easter

Holy Week

Monday

Ḥow Sweet Is the Cross

> O Lady, tell me where did you then stand—
> was it near the Cross? No, you were on the
> Cross itself, crucified with your Son.
> —St. Bonaventure

The path most fraught with anguish for Our Lady was the Via Dolorosa, where she walked in the footsteps of her beloved Son. What solace could we offer her? She witnessed the soldiers' brutality toward him, unable to ease his suffering as she stood by the Cross. John and Mary Magdalene stood by her, offering support, yet their grief mirrored hers.

In this letter dated July 1, 1915, Padre Pio observed to Padre Agostino that the word *cross* was sweet but Our Lady's sorrow was immense. He asked Our Lady to obtain graces for us from her most holy Son that we may more deeply penetrate the mysteries of the Cross.

My very dear Father,

May Jesus fill your soul with His choicest graces and enable you to experience more and more the happiness of the cross when carried with a Christian spirit.

How sweet is the word "cross!" Here at the foot of Jesus's cross souls are clothed in light and inflamed with love; here they acquire wings to bear them upwards in loftiest flight. May the same cross always be our bed of rest, our school of perfection, our beloved heritage. For this reason, we must never separate the cross from Jesus's love; otherwise it would become a weight which, in our weakness, we could not carry.

May the Sorrowful Virgin obtain for us from her most holy son the grace to penetrate more deeply into the mystery of the cross and, like her, to become inebriated with Jesus's suffering. The surest sign of love is the capacity to suffer for the beloved, and since the Son of God endured many sufferings for pure love, there is no doubt that the cross carried for him becomes as lovable as love itself. . . .

We must make every effort, like many elect souls, to follow invariably this Blessed Mother, to walk close to her since there is no other path leading to life. . . . Let us not refuse to take this path, we who want to reach our journey's end.

Let us invariably unite with this dear Mother. With her, close to Jesus, let us go out from Jerusalem . . . this manifestly faithless Jerusalem. Side by side with Jesus, let us go out into the open country, carrying with Him the glorious infamy of his Cross. The apostle invites us to do this: "Therefore let us go forth to him outside the camp, bearing abuse for him." The divine master also invites us: "If any man would come after me, let him deny himself and take up his cross and follow me." We must keep our eyes fixed on the noble, majestic and holy company of those who follow Jesus to Golgotha. Each one of them without exception bears the profession of the true faith on his countenance, self-denial in his heart, and the cross on his shoulders. Let us follow this courageous group for whom all consolations accompany every sacrifice and all hope is united with every virtue.

The enemy of our salvation knows only too well that peace of heart is a sure sign of the divine assistance, and hence he lets slip no opportunity to make us lose this peace. We must therefore always be on our guard in this respect. Jesus will help us. (*Letters I*, 674)

Reflect

Let us reflect on the words of Paul the Apostle. He urges, "Let us then go to him outside the camp, bearing the reproach that he bore" (Heb 13:13). The divine master also calls us: "Whoever wishes to come after me must deny himself, take up his cross, and follow me" (Mt 16:24).

We must fix our gaze on the noble assembly following Jesus to Golgotha. As we read above, each bears the true faith on their face, self-denial in their heart, and the Cross on their shoulders. Let us join this brave company, where every sacrifice is met with consolation, and every virtue is embraced with hope. Reflect on Padre Pio's words:

> May the Most Holy Virgin, who was the first to practice the gospel perfectly in all its severity, even before it was proclaimed, spur us on to follow closely in her footsteps.[1]

Christ, My Redeemer . . .

We follow Padre Pio to the Cross where we will stand close to Our Lady and comfort her in her untold grief! Amen.

Conclude your time of reflection and prayer with one Our Father, one Hail Mary, and one Glory Be.

Tuesday

In Search of the Compassionate Cyrenean

> And as they led him away, they seized one Simon of Cyrene, who was coming in from the country, and laid on him the cross, to carry it behind Jesus.
>
> —Luke 23:26

What significance does my love hold in the sight of God? **Padre Pio** asks Padre Agostino this question in his letter dated April 21, 1915. He was deeply troubled by the notion that his affection for God may not be genuine. This fear was just one among his many agonies that left him feeling utterly overwhelmed. Yet, he told Padre Agostino that he possessed a profound longing to endure suffering out of love for Jesus.

So, he questioned why it is that, faced with trials, he found himself instinctively seeking relief against his will? What inner resolve and fortitude must he draw upon to put an end to the natural instinct that craved comfort? For answers, he turned to the story of Simon of Cyrene, who comforted the Lord on his own via dolorosa (see Matthew 27:32).

> My very dear Father.
>
> Praise be to Jesus! Your last letter brought a little consolation to my extremely afflicted spirit. . . . I know quite well that the cross is a token of love, down payment of forgiveness, and that love which is not fed and nourished by the cross is not true love but merely a flash in the pan. Yet in spite of this knowledge, this false disciple of the Nazarene feels the cross weighing enormously on his heart and very often (don't be scandalized or horrified, Father, by what I am about to say) he goes in search of the compassionate Cyrenean who relieves and comforts him.
>
> What value can this love of mine have with God? I am very much afraid on this account that, my love of God is not true love. This is one of the many torments which, combined with many more, overwhelm me to the point where I feel utterly crushed.
>
> Still, my dear Father, I have a great desire to suffer for the love of Jesus. How is it, then, that when I am put to the test, altogether against my will I seek relief? What force and violence must I use towards myself in these trials to reduce nature to silence when it cries out loudly, so to speak, for consolation? (*Letters I*, 639)

In his responding letter, dated May 2, 1915, Padre Agostino reminded Padre Pio of the reality of Christ's suffering—that at times the spirit is willing, but the flesh is weak!

My beloved son in Jesus Christ.

You asked me for an explanation of the way you are suffering, and you told me that you often go in search of the Cyrenean, that nature cries out for relief and hence it seems to you that your love for God is not sincere and perfect.

This is an illusion, my son! . . . In point of fact, during his voluntary agony Jesus prayed in his human nature for the chalice to be taken away and the heavenly Father sent an Angel to comfort him! At times the spirit is willing, but the flesh is weak! But God wants the spirit, not the flesh.

Let nature complain then; your will, with God's help, will remain the master and divine love will never diminish in your soul. . . . While God tries us by His crosses and suffering, He always leaves a glimmer of light in our hearts, by which we continue to have great trust in Him and to behold His immense goodness. (*Letters I*, 642)

Reflect

Are you like Simon of Cyrene, allowing the soldiers to place the Cross of Jesus on your shoulders? Are you like Padre Pio, willing to join Jesus to make reparation for the sins of all men? Would you be willing to relieve Jesus one moment of his suffering? Reflect on the words of Padre Pio:

Our Lord sometimes makes you feel the weight of the cross. This weight seems unbearable, but you carry it because in His love and mercy, the Lord helps you and gives you strength.[2]

Christ, My Redeemer ...

Grant me the strength to bear the weight of the Cross alongside you as Padre Pio did, offering relief and joining in reparation for all concealed sins. Amen.

Conclude your time of reflection and prayer with one Our Father, one Hail Mary, and one Glory Be.

My Body Is All Bruised

The enemy will be beaten.

—Padre Agostino

As we enter into the final day of Lent, just before the Triduum, we anticipate the horrors that are in store for Christ as he takes upon himself the sins of the world in his decisive battle against the powers of darkness. And once more, ever the faithful son, Padre Pio follows in the footsteps of Christ and lays his body down, willingly suffering in union with his Redeemer. On February 13, 1913, Padre Pio wrote in his letter to Padre Agostino that Jesus allowed the evil one to vent his anger on him for twenty-two days, causing great harm to his body.

My dear Father,

I'm very happy just now. Jesus never stops loving me in spite of all my shortcomings, for he allows those ugly face creatures to afflict me incessantly. For the past twenty-two days Jesus has allowed them to vent their anger on me continually. My body, dear father, is bruised all over, from all the blows it has received at the hands of our enemies.

More than once they even went so far as to pull off my night shirt and beat me in that state. Tell me, now, was it not Jesus who helped me in those awful moments when I was bereft of all other assistance and the devils tried to destroy my body and soul? Add to this that even when they were through, I remained stripped for quite a long time as I was powerless to move, and this in the present severely cold season. How much harm would they have done me if our most tender Jesus had not come to my assistance!

I know only one thing for certain, that the Lord will never fall short of his promises. "Do not fear, I will make you suffer, but I will also give you the strength to suffer," Jesus tells me continually. "I want your soul to be purified and tried by a daily hidden martyrdom; do not be frightened if I allow the devil to torment you, the world to disgust you, and your nearest and dearest to afflict you, for nothing will prevail against those who groan beneath the Cross for love of me and whom I have taken care to protect. . . . Beneath the Cross one learns to love, and I do not grant this to everyone, but only to those who are dearest to me." (*Letters I*, 381)

Padre Agostino responded to Padre Pio on February 27, 1913.

My beloved son in Jesus Christ . . .

I cannot tell you how it consoles me to know of your happiness: your joy is mine. May Jesus be forever blessed for what he is doing to you continually. Courage, my son, the enemy will be confounded and vanquished!

May I ask you to recommend me also to our dear heavenly Mother. Oh, how good she is! (*Letters I*, 383)

Reflect

Do we feel the strength of the Lord when we entrust him with our suffering? Do we stand beneath his Cross and share his suffering?

The Lord says, "Do not be frightened if I allow the devil to torment you, the world to disgust you, and your nearest and dearest to afflict you." The Lord will protect us as he protected Padre Pio. Reflect on the words of Padre Pio:

> The more you are afflicted, the more you ought to rejoice, because in the fire of tribulation the soul will become pure gold, worthy to be placed and to shine in the heavenly palace.[3]

Christ, My Redeemer . . .

On this journey, let us learn how to surrender all to you. Amen.

Conclude your time of reflection and prayer with one Our Father, one Hail Mary, and one Glory Be.

I Spent the Night in the Passion with Our Lord

> The death and passion of Our Lord is the
> sweetest and most constraining motive that
> can animate our hearts in this mortal life . . .
> so, in the glory of heaven above, next to the
> Divine goodness known and considered in
> itself, Our Savior's death shall most powerfully
> ravish the blessed spirits in the loving of God.
> —St. Francis de Sales

In his letter dated June 28, 1912, Padre Pio told Padre Agostino that Jesus shared his Passion with him in a most unexpected way—not simply as a man, but as a child as well—his most trusted friend.

My dear Father,

I had a very bad time the night before last; from about ten o'clock, when I went to bed, until five in the morning, that wretch did nothing but beat me continually. He presented to my mind many diabolical suggestions, thoughts of despair, distrust in God. But praise be to Jesus, for I defended myself by saying to him repeatedly: your words are my merit.

I really thought that was the last night of my life, or that if I did not die, I should lose my reason. But may Jesus be blessed, for nothing of the sort occurred.

At five in the morning, when that wretch left me, my whole body became so cold that I trembled from head to foot like a reed exposed to a violent wind. This lasted for a couple of hours. I spat blood. In the end the infant Jesus came to me, to whom I said I only wanted to do his will. Dear God! How my heart throbbed, how my cheeks burned while this heavenly Child was close to me!

Then, last night, I spent the entire night with Jesus in his Passion. I also suffered a great deal, but in a very different way from the previous night. This was his suffering which did me absolutely no harm. My trust in God increased more and more and I felt increasingly attracted towards Jesus. Although there was no fire nearby, I felt myself burning within; although there were no bonds, I felt myself tightly bound to Jesus. I burned with one thousand flames which made me live and die at the same time. Hence, I suffered, lived and died continually.

Dear Father, if I could fly, I would like to shout, to cry out to everyone at the top of my voice: love Jesus who is deserving of love. But, alas, my dear Father, my soul is still strongly bound to the body, and many are the sins which impede the flight of my soul.

Pray that the Lord may be pleased to shorten my exile. Explain to me the origin of this blind desire I have to depart from this life. My sins are many and they ought to check my blind passion. I ponder over them yet feel more and more attracted by the desire to take flight from the world. (*Letters I*, 329)

Reflect

This letter vividly portrayed the physical anguish—trembling and even spitting blood—representing the profound spiritual struggle Padre Pio endured. Yet, amid this suffering, a transformative moment of grace occurred: the "infant Jesus" appeared, offering comfort and strengthening Pio's faith.

Padre Pio recounted a night immersed in contemplation of Jesus's Passion. Unlike the saint's previous suffering, this was a communion with Jesus's own pain, deepening his trust in God, and enhancing his spiritual connection. Despite these intense spiritual experiences, Padre Pio longed to depart this life ("shorten my exile"). This arose from his yearning for deeper union with God and the profound disconnection he felt between the spiritual and earthly realms.

Padre Pio acknowledged his own sins as obstacles and felt a compelling draw toward spiritual liberation. This inner conflict—between earthly imperfections and spiritual aspirations—was his struggle for purity and closeness to God.

Padre Pio's journey mirrored spiritual highs and lows, where suffering and temptation were countered by moments of profound spiritual unity and divine grace. His writings reveal the complexities of faith, the struggle against sin, and the enduring yearning for spiritual transcendence.

Do we feel the strength of the Lord when we entrust him with our suffering? Do we stand beneath the Cross and share his suffering?

Reflect on Padre Pio's words:

My heart brims with bitterness, yet I accept [the Stigmata] as the affectionate will of Jesus.[4]

Christ, My Redeemer . . .

As we kneel near you in the Garden of Gethsemane, we pray: Jesus, may we always allow ourselves to be shaped by your divine hands. May we surrender to you, allowing you to work within us. Let us not interpret everything merely in a human sense but accept your divine intervention. Let us surrender ourselves to your embrace as though lifeless, ready to endure whatever trials you arrange for our sanctification. Let us embrace everything that you inspire within us for the honor and glory of your Father. Amen.

Conclude your time of reflection and prayer with one Our Father, one Hail Mary, and one Glory Be.

Good Friday

A Great Vision of Jesus

> I weep over the sorrows and disgraces of my
> Lord: and what causes me the greatest sorrow
> is, that men, for whom he suffered so much,
> live in forgetfulness of him.
> —St. Francis of Assisi

In his letter to Padre Agostino dated March 12, 1913, Padre Pio reflected on Jesus's justified grievances. Jesus expressed his disappointment to Padre Pio and lamented the ingratitude of humanity despite his profound love for them.

> Listen, my dear Father, to the justified complaints of our most sweet Jesus: "With what ingratitude is my love for men repaid! I should be less offended by them if I had loved them less. My Father does not want to bear with them any longer. I myself want to stop loving them, but. . . . (here Jesus paused, sighed, then continued) but, alas! My heart is made to love! Weak and cowardly men make no effort to overcome temptation and indeed they take delight in their wickedness. The souls for whom I have a special predilection fail me when put to the test, the weak give way to discour-

agement and despair, while the strong are relaxing by
degrees.

They leave me alone by night, alone by day, and in
the churches. They no longer care about the Sacrament
of the Altar. Hardly anyone speaks of the Sacrament of
Love, and even those who do speak, alas, do so with
great indifference and coldness.

My heart is forgotten! Nobody thinks anymore
of My love, and I am continually grieved. Even my
ministers, whom I loved as the apple of my eye, who
ought to console my heart brimming over with sorrow,
who ought to assist me in the redemption of souls, who
would believe it!" (*Letters I*, 385–386)

In his letter dated April 7, 1913, Padre Pio told Padre Agostino
a great vision he had of Jesus. In this vision, Jesus elaborated on
all that he told Padre Pio about the ingratitude of men.

My very dear Father,

On Friday morning while I was still in bed, Jesus
appeared to me. He was in a sorry state and quite dis-
figured. He showed me a great multitude of priests,
regular and secular, among whom were several high
ecclesiastical dignitaries. Some were celebrating Mass
while others were vesting or taking off the sacred vest-
ments.

The sight of Jesus in distress was very painful to
me, so I asked him why he was suffering so much.
There was no reply, but his gaze turned on the priests.
Shortly afterwards, as if terrified and weary of looking at them, he withdrew His gaze. Then He raised
his eyes and looked at me and to my great horror I

observed two tears coursing down his cheeks. He drew back from the crowd of priests with an expression of great disgust on his face and cried out: "Butchers!" Then turning to me he said: "My son, do not think that My agony lasted three hours. No, on account of the souls who have received most from me, I shall be in agony until the end of the world. During my agony, my son, nobody should sleep. My soul goes in search of a drop of human compassion but alas, I am left alone beneath the weight of indifference. The ingratitude and the sleep of my ministers makes my agony all the more grievous.

"Alas, how little they correspond to my love! What afflicts me most is that they add contempt and unbelief to their indifference. Many times, I have been on the point of annihilating them, had I not been held back by the Angels and by souls who are filled with love for me. . . ."

Jesus continued to speak but what he said I can never reveal to any creature in this world. This apparition caused me such bodily pain and the even greater pain of soul that I was prostate for the entire day and believed I should die of this suffering, had our most sweet Jesus not revealed to me . . .[5] (*Letters I*, 385)

Reflect

Each of our sins is a thorn that deeply wounds the Lord's sacred brow. Oh, the crown of thorns they will place upon you! How many crowns of thorns do the evil thoughts of humanity press upon your beloved head, until your blood flows onto your beautiful face! Reflect on the words of Padre Pio:

> Imagine Jesus crucified in your arms and on your chest and say a hundred times as you kiss His chest, "This is my hope, the living source of my happiness; this is the heart of my soul; nothing will ever separate me from His love."[6]

Christ, My Redeemer . . .

On this Good Friday, I ask that you keep me eternally near to you. Never allow us to be separated, not even for an instant. Instead, grant me the privilege to console you, to atone for any wrongdoing against you, and to offer solace on behalf of all, for I sense the immense weight of sins burdening you in every form. Amen.

Conclude your time of reflection and prayer with one Our Father, one Hail Mary, and one Glory Be.

Holy Saturday

A Sign of Hope

> Live in faith and hope, though it be in darkness, for in this darkness God protects the soul. Cast your care upon God for you are His and He will not forget you. Do not think that He is leaving you alone, for that would be to wrong Him.
>
> —St. John of the Cross

Come with me back to the first Holy Week. It is the morning after the first night of Passover. The events of Good Friday have left the city in silent turmoil. Many of the followers of Jesus have retreated to their homes and remain there behind locked doors.

We follow Padre Pio on the path from Calvary to the Tomb. In the silence of the morning, we find the soldiers guarding the Tomb of Our Lord and Redeemer. He has not yet ascended into heaven. As we approach the Tomb, we listen to the words of Padre Pio to Padre Agostino, delivering in this beautiful letter dated October 17, 1915, a message of hope.

> Oh, dear Jesus, never let me lose this precious treasure that you are for me. My Lord and my God, I experi-

ence, too vividly in my soul, the ineffable tenderness
that pours forth from your eyes, the love with which
you, my only Good, condescend to gaze on this mis-
erable creature.

How can the torment of my heart be placated, the
agony of knowing I am far from you? My soul is well
aware of the terrible battle I endured when you, O
my Beloved, hid yourself from me! Oh my most tender Lover, how clearly is this terrible and frightening
image imprinted on my soul!

Who will ever be capable of eliminating or extin-
guishing the ardent flames of this fire which burns in
my breast for you? Ah, Lord, do not take pleasure in
hiding yourself; you know what confusion and turmoil
this causes in all the faculties of my soul and in all my
feelings! You see that my soul cannot bear the cruel
torment of this abandonment, for you have enchanted
it too much, oh infinite Beauty!

You know how anxiously my soul seeks you. This
anxiety is no less than that of your spouse in the sacred
Songs; my soul, too, like that holy spouse, wanders in
the public streets and in the squares and adjures the
daughters of Jerusalem to tell her where her Beloved
is: "I adjure you, O daughters of Jerusalem, if you find
my beloved, that you tell him I am sick with love . . ."

Oh holy souls free from all anxiety, who are
already made happy in heaven by that torrent of
supreme sweetness, how I envy you your happiness!
Ah, for pity's sake, since you are so close to the Fountain of Life, since you see me dying of thirst in this

despicable world, be propitious to me and give me a little of that delightful freshwater.

You exhort me to offer myself as a victim to the Lord for poor sinners. I made this offering once and I renew it several times a day. But how is it that the Lord does not hear me? I also offered my life for the salvation of sinners, yet the Lord still sustains me in life.

Above all, let us humble ourselves at all times before the majesty of the Lord, from whose presence we must endeavor never to withdraw. And let us always be on guard not to let the devil creep in through the abominable vice of vainglory. . . . I recommend my poor soul to you, with the souls of all those I have at heart. (*Letters I*, 754)

Reflect

To grasp the essence of the Lord's love for us and the love of Padre Pio for the Lord, one need only immerse themselves in the exquisite words written by Padre Pio in this letter. As Holy Saturday morning unfolds it calls us to set aside all distractions and contemplate the events of recent days, particularly the profound sacrifice Our Lord undertook for us. It's a moment to ponder deeply on the magnitude of His love for us.

Reflect further on Padre Pio's words:

May Jesus continue to keep his Fatherly gaze fixed on you; May he always sustain you in grace and help you to fight the good fight, making you share in the reward of strong souls. (*Letters I*, 751)

Christ, My Redeemer . . .

As we approach your Tomb, let us reflect on those wonderful days of Lent we spent with Padre Pio and how we
have enriched our spiritual life through his inspiration.
Amen.

*Conclude your time of reflection and prayer with one Our
Father, one Hail Mary, and one Glory Be.*

Easter Sunday

Christ Is Risen

The very first Easter taught us this: that life
never ends and love never dies.

—Kate McGahan

God the Father sent his only begotten Son, Jesus Christ,
born of Mary, to deliver the world from sin and death.
Through his Crucifixion and Resurrection, Christ recon-
ciled us with God, conquered death, and shattered Satan's
dominion. This act stands as the ultimate sacrifice for
humanity.

Who could ever repay the Lord for this profound
sacrifice?

During Lent, we traveled the road to Calvary under
the guidance of Padre Pio. For fifty years, Padre Pio bore
the Stigmata and suffered Christ's Passion and Death daily.

Padre Pio's solace during those years when he battled
with the devil came from the letters he exchanged with
mentor priests—a distraction vital to his perseverance,
a way to channel his mission, and for us, a gateway into
his essence. In retracing his steps, we found words that
resonated deep within our hearts.

In excerpts from a letter dated January 12, 1919, Padre Pio told Padre Benedetto how encountering divine love was like going through a big transformation that could be both challenging and beautiful, bringing us closer to God even when it feels tough.

> My dear Father,
>
> I tremble once more as I write to you! But why do I tremble? I find it almost impossible to explain the action of the Beloved. In the immensity of his strength, Infinite love has at last overcome my hard-heartedness, leaving me weak and powerless. . . .
>
> How can I carry the Infinite in this little heart of mine? How can I continue to confine him to the narrow cell of my soul? My soul is melting with pain and love, with bitterness and sweetness simultaneously.
>
> The embraces of my Beloved which follow one another and with great profusion, I should say incessantly, immeasurably and unsparingly, cannot extinguish in my soul the acute pain caused by my inadequacy to bear the weight of an infinite love. It is precisely during these periods which are almost continuous that my soul utters phrases to the divine Lover which horrify me when I am in my right mind. (*Letters I*, 1238)

In an Easter letter dated April 13, 1919, Padre Agostino illustrated how Padre Pio's mission fostered a deepening of faith, a readiness to impart spiritual blessings to others, and a firm trust in God's design for salvation and everlasting life.

Beloved son in Jesus Christ,

May Jesus be always yours and transform you fully into himself until you possess him entirely in heavenly glory. This is my wish for you during this holy Easter feast. Jesus is now crucified in you, and you are crucified in Him. His passion is the continual food of your soul and indeed can and must exclaim with St. Paul and with our Seraphic Father: I bear on my body the marks of Jesus! But always remember that the gifts of God, freely given, are also intended for the sanctification of others.

Say in favor of all the souls when Jesus has confided to you: The grace of our Lord be with your spirit, brethren. Amen! May my own soul be among the number of these, and may the divine will be always accomplished in me, through me and by me. You know the needs of all, and Jesus has given you the power to provide a remedy for them. Make use, therefore, of the great condescension Jesus shows you for the benefit and salvation of our souls.

During these days you will experience more keenly the passion of Jesus in your spirit and in your flesh. May he also allow you to share in the joy of his glorious resurrection. . . . Nothing is lacking to you now except eternal paradise, and this will undoubtedly come when it pleases God and holy obedience. I bless you and ask your prayers. (*Letters I*, 1265)

Reflect

Padre Pio showed us how experiencing God's love could be intense and overwhelming. It's like feeling a mix of emotions all at once, like love and pain, and it can make you feel weak and unsure. He also mentioned how it is hard to fully understand how much God loves us and how that love can change us.

Do you let Jesus act in you as he pleases, in the certainty that all is according to his will? Do you surrender all to the will of Jesus? Do you trust him to do all that is good for you? Do you give it all to the Lord? Reflect on Padre Pio's words:

> May Jesus be always with you, and may He be pleased to make all redeemed souls worthy to be received one day into the kingdom of glory. May He include us in the great number of those who have known how to make continual progress at the school of His love.[7]

Christ, My Redeemer . . .

May the Holy Spirit fill your soul with his most holy gifts and make you holy. May the risen Jesus reign within your soul forever. Amen.

Conclude your time of reflection and prayer with one Our Father, one Hail Mary, and one Glory Be.

Notes

All for the Love of His Childhood Companion: Week of Ash Wednesday

1. Pio of Pietrelcina to Antonietta Vona, 1918, quoted in "Lent with Padre Pio: Ash Wednesday," *Franciscan Spirit Blog*, March 2, 2022, https://www.franciscanmedia.org/franciscan-spirit-blog/lent-with-padre-pio-ash-wednesday.

2. Pio of Pietrelcina, in *Letters I: Correspondence with His Spiritual Directors, 1910–1922*, ed. Gerardo di Flumeri (San Giovanni Rotondo, Italy: Our Lady of Grace Capuchin Friary, 1980), 800, quoted in José Saraiva Martins, "Padre Pio: One with Christ, One with Sinners," EWTN, https://www.ewtn.com/catholicism/library/padre-pio-one-with-christ-one-with-sinners-13845.

3. Pio of Pietrelcina, March 1948, in *Letters I*, quoted in José Saraiva Martins, "Padre Pio: One with Christ, One with Sinners," ETWN, https://www.ewtn.com/catholicism/library/padre-pio-one-with-christ-one-with-sinners-13845.

4. See book X of Augustine of Hippo's *Confessions*.

5. The Voice of Padre Pio, Facebook, September 25, 2017, https://www.facebook.com/saintpadrepio/posts/

fbid02QqU1E7R8ZPJh1Bad5Nzwq9a3nURXB4URVN-JXmCaaciPjNLs93a9QvF9TcdEex9pBl.

6. Pio of Pietrelcina to Raffaelina, 1914, in *Epistolario II: Corrispondenza con la nobildonna Raffaelina Cerase, 1914–1915*, ed. Melchiorre da Probladura and Alessandro da Ripabottoni (San Giovanni Rotondo, Italy: Our Lady of Grace Capuchin Friary, 1975), 403, quoted in William Wagner, "Padre Pio and the Guardian Angel," *Opus Sanctorum Angelorum*, 2021, https://opusangelorum.org/padre-pio-and-the-guardian-angel.

7. One of the ways the devil tried to thwart Padre Pio was tempting him not to read his spiritual director's letters—or defacing the letters so they could not be read without divine intervention!

8. Pio of Pietrelcina, quoted in Maura Roan McKeegan, "Padre Pio & the Friendship of Guardian Angels in Times of Need," *Catholic Exchange*, April 9, 2020, https://catholicexchange.com/padre-pio-and-the-friendship-of-guardian-angels-in-times-of-need.

9. Louis Solcia, "Padre Pio's Love for the Blessed Mother," Padre Pio Devotions, https://padrepiodevotions.org/pray-hope-and-dont-worry-issue-21-july-september-2004.

10. G. K. Chesterton, quoted in *Wisdom of the Day* (blog), *Aleteia*, October 31, 2017, https://aleteia.org/2017/10/31/each-generation-is-converted-by-the-saint-who-contradicts-it-most.

11. Frank Rega, "Walk Cheerfully!": Practical Advice from St. Padre Pio," *The Shield of Faith* (blog), September 2, 2014, https://divinefiat.blogspot.com/2014/09/walk-cheerfully-practical-advice-from.html.

12. Catherine Birri, "The Greatest Quotes from the Amazing Padre Pio," *Cora Evans Blog*, The Mystical Humanity of Christ Publishing, https://www.coraevans.com/blog/article/the-greatest-quotes-from-the-amazing-padre-pio.

13. "Padre Pio Quotes about Heaven," *Quotes* (blog), Vatican Site Pro Life, May 1, 2017, https://www.vaticansite.com/padre-pio-quotes-heaven.

The Invisible Stigmata: Second Week of Lent

1. "Padre Pio Quotes on the Virgin Mary," *Quotes* (blog), Vatican Site Pro Life, May 3, 2017, https://www.vaticansite.com/padre-pio-quotes-blessed-virgin-mary.

2. Padre Pio's statement emphasizes a theological perspective in which enduring suffering is seen not as a weakening of faith but as a chance to strengthen one's trust in God and look forward to spiritual liberation. It reflects the belief that suffering can be redemptive, fostering spiritual growth and offering release from the constraints of physical existence.

3. "216 Spiritual Quotes from St. Padre Pio for Your Personal Meditation," Catholics Striving for Holiness, September 23, 2015, https://catholicsstrivingforholiness.org/sept-23-216-spiritual-maxims-from-padre-pio-for-your-meditation.

4. Pio of Pietrelcina, "Prayer of Surrender to Jesus," quoted in "St. Padre Pio Prayers," Padre Pio Ministry to the Suffering, https://padrepioministry.org/padre-pio-prayers.

5. Years later, in 1918, when news circulated that Padre Pio bore the Stigmata, Pannullo confirmed his earlier witnessing of the wounds. "You see them now," he remarked. "I saw them in 1910."

6. Bernard Ruffin, *Padre Pio: The True Story*, quoted in "Why Padre Pio Thought Suffering Was a Blessing from God," Ave Maria Radio, accessed August 15, 2024, https://avemariaradio.net/why-padre-pio-thought-suffering-was-a-blessing-from-god.

7. "Padre Pio Quotes about Suffering" *Quotes* (blog), Vatican Site Pro Life, May 3, 2017, https://www.vatican-site.com/padre-pio-quotes-suffering.

8. Pio of Pietrelcina, in *Letters III: Correspondence with His Spiritual Daughters, 1915–1923*, ed. Gerardo de Flumeri (San Giovanni Rotondo, Italy: Our Lady of Grace Capuchin Friary, 1980), quoted in "Padre Pio's Letter to His Spiritual Daughter," Saints' Works, July 12, 2024, https://www.saintsworks.net/Modesty%20and%20Purity%20-%20Padre%20Pio's%20Letter%20to%20His%20Spiritual%20Daughter.html.

9. Pio of Pietrelcina, *Letters III*, 84.

Demons All Around Me: Third Week of Lent

1. Philip Kosloski, "Padre Pio Prayed This Prayer to the Virgin Mary Every First Saturday," *Aleteia*, June 9, 2018, https://aleteia.org/2018/06/09/padre-pio-prayed-this-prayer-to-the-virgin-mary-every-first-saturday.

2. Padre Benedetto is emphasizing the importance of recognizing and accepting the divine will in all events of life. He suggests that every event, whether perceived as positive or negative, is part of a greater divine plan. By acknowledging this, believers can find meaning and purpose in their experiences, even when those experiences are difficult.

3. Maria Cintorino, "Pray, Hope and Don't Worry: Learning from Padre Pio's Words of Wisdom," *Life & Culture* (blog), Busted Halo, September 22, 2023, https://bustedhalo.com/life-culture/pray-hope-and-dont-worry-learning-from-padre-pios-words-of-wisdom.

4. "Happy Feast of St. Padre Pio!" CatholicsCome-Home.org, https://www.catholicscomehome.org/happy-feast-of-st-padre-pio.

5. "Spiritual Advice from Padre Pio," Saint Benedict Center, accessed August 15, 2024, https://www.saintbenedict.com/catholic-resources/spiritual-advice-from-padre-pio.

6. Laura Williamson, "Padre Pio: In His Own Words," Catholic Truth, May 12, 2024, https://catholictruth.org/padre-pio-in-his-own-words.

7. "Padre Pio's Advice on Guardian Angels," America Needs Fatima, accessed August 15, 2024, https://americaneedsfatima.org/prayers/padre-pios-advice-on-guardian-angels.

Mystical Touches: Fourth Week of Lent

1. "Ten Quotes from Padre Pio on the Blessed Virgin Mary," Ave Maria Radio, accessed August 15, 2024, https://avemariaradio.net/10-quotes-from-padre-pio-on-the-blessed-virgin-mary.

2. Pio of Pietrelcina, quoted in "We Don't Just Receive," The Divine Mercy, https://www.thedivinemercy.org/articles/we-dont-just-receive-0.

3. "Padre Pio Quotes on Spiritual Warfare," *Quotes* (blog), Vatican Site Pro Life, May 1, 2017, https://www.vaticansite.com/padre-pio-quotes-spiritual-warfare.

4. "St. Padre Pio's Prayer of Thanksgiving after Mass," St. Thomas the Apostle Parish, accessed August 22, 2024, https://statucson.org/st-padre-pios-prayer-of-thanksgiving-after-mass.

5. Pierino Galeone, "Padre Pio's Experience and Testimony of God's Sanctity," (unpublished manuscript, July 28, 2018), Microsoft Word binary file.

Padre Pio's Stigmata: Fifth Week of Lent

1. "Padre Pio's Words of Faith," Padre Pio Devotions, accessed August 16, 2024, https://padrepiodevotions.org/st-pio.

2. "Saint Padre Pio Quotes," *The Catholic Reader* (blog), June 2, 2013, https://thecatholicreader.blogspot.com/2013/06/saint-padre-pio-quotes.html.

3. For more information on this period in Padre Pio's life, read *The Pandemic of Padre Pio: Disciple of Our Lady of Sorrows* by Stefano Campenella; Bret Thoman, "How Padre Pio Responded When Asked about the Spanish Influenza Pandemic," *Catholic365* (blog), March 26, 2021, https://www.catholic365.com/article/12295/how-padre-pio-responded-when-asked-about-the-spanish-influenza-pandemic.html.

4. Whitney Hopler, "Send Me Your Angels: St. Padre Pio and the Guardian Angels," Learn Religions, December 1, 2017, https://www.learnreligions.com/saint-padre-pio-and-guardian-angels-3987792.

Carry the Cross toward Easter: Holy Week

1. "Padre Pio Quotes on the Blessed Virgin Mary," *Quotes* (blog), Vatican Site Pro Life, May 3, 2017, https://www.vaticansite.com/padre-pio-quotes-blessed-virgin-mary.

2. "Quotes by Padre Pio about the Cross of Jesus Christ," Vatican Site Pro Life, May 1, 2017, https://www.vaticansite.com/quotes-padre-pio-cross-jesus-christ.

3. Melissa Guerrero, "Tough Love and Wisdom from the Words of St. Pio of Pietrelcina," *Epic Pew* (blog), September 26, 2019, https://epicpew.com/tough-love-and-wisdom-from-the-words-of-st-pio-of-pietrelcina.

4. "Embracing the Cross: Lessons from St. Padre Pio's Life of Suffering," *Laudate Miriam* (blog), August 8, 2023, https://laudate-mariam.com/blogs/laudate-mariam-blog/embracing-the-cross-lessons-from-st-padre-pios-life-of-suffering.

5. Note: Padre Pio left a blank here. It is not possible to identify the subject of this revelation.

6. "Quotes by Padre Pio about the Cross of Jesus Christ," *Quotes* (blog), Vatican Site Pro Life, May 1, 2017, https://www.vaticansite.com/quotes-padre-pio-cross-jesus-christ.

7. "Padre Pio Quotes about Jesus," *Quotes* (blog), Vatican Site Pro Life, May 3, 2017, https://www.vaticansite.com/padre-pio-quotes-jesus.

Susan De Bartoli is the author of the award-winning *Welcoming the Christ Child with Padre Pio* and *Welcoming the Holy Spirit with Padre Pio*. She serves as the secretary of the Board of Directors of the Padre Pio Foundation of America, assists with the Cause for Canonization of Mary Pyle (Padre Pio's assistant), and owns Little Flower Pilgrimages.

De Bartoli has been a guest on various radio and television shows and podcasts, including *Let's Be Frank*, *Seize the Day* with Gus Lloyd, EWTN's *Catholic Connection* with Teresa Tomeo, and *Catholic Faith Network Live*.

She is a lady commander of the Equestrian Order of the Holy Sepulchre of Jerusalem. She lives in the New York area.

littleflowerpilgrimages.com
Facebook: @susan.debartoli
Instagram: @susan_debartoli

Cardinal Timothy M. Dolan is the archbishop of New York. In 2012, Pope Benedict XVI announced that Cardinal Dolan was to be appointed to the College of Cardinals.

ALSO BY
SUSAN DE BARTOLI

Welcoming the Christ Child with Padre Pio
offers stories about the saint woven with scripture
and prayer to help you experience Advent—
Padre Pio's favorite season—with greater hope and joy.
Each day includes daily readings, a quotation
from Padre Pio, a short story about the saint,
a scripture reflection, and a prayer to help you follow
this extraordinary saint's example and welcome the Christ Child
into your home and heart during Advent.

Welcoming the Holy Spirit with Padre Pio
shares stories and wisdom from the life
of this humble monk to show how we can use
our unique spiritual gifts to love others and draw
from the well of faith to encounter Christ
in profound ways.